At the Crossroads of Der Zor

Death, Survival, and Humanitarian
Resistance in Aleppo, 1915-1917

Hilmar Kaiser

in collaboration with
Luther and Nancy Eskijian

At the Crossroads of Der Zor was originally printed as a special publication by the Gomidas Institute. The success of that edition has led to the present edition for general release.

Illustration Credits
Eskijian Family Archives (pp. 7, 39, 41, 43, 45, 75), German Foreign Office Archives, Berlin (pp. 47, 49, 63), Ara Sarafian (p. vii)

Front cover design by Katya Danailova. Front cover photo from the Eskijian family archives.

Printed in the United States of America

ISBN   978-1-940145-72-3 (paperback)
            978-1-940145-73-0 (ebook)

This edition of *At the Crossroads of Der Zor* is published by Signalman Publishing with the permission of Gomidas Institute Books. For inquiries, contact:
Signalman Publishing
Tampa, Florida
Email: info@signalmanpublishing.com

Contents

PREFACE—ONE HUNDRED YEARS AGO 1915-2015

My life has been deeply affected by a man I never met, and one who died at the age of 34 years old. That man, Rev. Hovhannes Eskijian, is the subject of this book, but I believe, if he were here today, he would simply say he was a servant, used by God at a critical time in the history of our nation. My grandmother, who labored alongside him, collected all the materials she could on him, and said someday it would be important, imparting that urgency to my father, Mr. Luther Eskijian. Perhaps today is that day, when, at the time of this writing, the same spiritual and political forces that operated to destroy the Armenian people and other Christians in Turkey one hundred years ago, are at work to annihilate Christians in the Middle East, Pakistan, the Sudan, Nigeria, Indonesia, among other places, and in the same brutal manner. Christians, and others, are beheaded, crucified, abducted, enslaved, raped, murdered, and tortured, and a refugee population is created again. There is nothing new under the sun.

In 2014 alone the Der Zor memorial to the Armenian Genocide in Syria, an area where hundreds of thousands died, was destroyed by the Islamic State (ISIS). Churches and ancient manuscripts have been destroyed and burned in Syria and Iraq, crosses broken, graves destroyed. Grandfather's grave in Aleppo was desecrated three times that I know of in the past. The first church Rev. Eskijian started to build as a pastor in the village of Ek-iz-oluk (which my father completed) was bombed by the Al Nusra front—an Al Qaeda faction. We know the plight of city of Kessab, the Armenian enclave; and Aleppo, where Rev. Eskijian served, became a war zone. And this is just a small picture of what is happening on a massive scale and history repeating itself.

The Genocide caused the death of 1.5 million Armenians, the dispersion of hundreds of thousands, including my father, grandmother, my uncle, his brother, and several relatives both from my mother's and father's side of the family, the creation of over a hundred thousand orphans many experiencing terrible fates, and a world of heinous crimes. I heard stories from my youngest years about miraculous escapes and tragedies. The Turks came three times to kill my young father and his remaining family. These narratives had impact on my view of life, as well as my siblings. We learned that life is serious and that massive pain can be inflicted, that our forefathers suffered greatly, and to be thankful for our safe, free and prosperous lives in the United States, using the opportunity to help others.

However, we also learned of the triumph of Rev. Eskijian's life in Christ, and the many who served with him in his underground efforts, in the middle of suffering and under great pressure, which you will read about in this book. Although I never met Rev. Eskijian, that doesn't mean I never knew him.

His character was founded in Christ: From an article by Rev. Elmajian who was assisted at his orphanage as a young man: "He was a patient, humble, affectionate man. All day long to everyone, good or bad, had a sweet word of comfort, with an angelic smile without hurting anyone. I used to watch this holy man who had a treasure in his heart to everyone. I never saw anger, impatience or complaint at any time. In his orphanage which he started, miraculously saving the poor orphans from the hand of Turks, he had no rest day or night. He forgot his home and sleep. Rev. Eskijian had not only saved Protestants, but whoever came to him Gregorian or Catholic."

His compassion was expressed in Christ: He opened three orphanages, according to my uncle, to save as many of the young as possible. He worked tirelessly to find any and all means to save another Armenian.

His courage was rooted in Christ: As he said in one of his messages as the dark clouds of war and Genocide fell on Aleppo: "Dear friends, be courageous. Let us die, but let no one deny his Lord. This honorable opportunity does not come to us often. I myself am ready for the gallows." He died of typhus the day before he was to be hanged.

His commitment was lived out through Christ: John Minassian, his young assistant, estimated that thousands of Armenians were saved from death by his efforts, and the efforts of those who joined him in this endeavor.

Sisag Manoogian, the priest of Chorum wrote, "I the undersigned priest of Chorum testify that whatever the Rev. H. Eskijian did to our nation, no one else did, neither a Catholicos, nor a national representative, God bless his soul."

Several years ago, and two generations later, I attended a conference for pastors in my church denomination in Jerusalem (I am a pastor of a church in Los Angeles). There were leaders from all over the world, including a Turkish pastor who had been mentioned at the conference because Muslim attackers killed three Christians from a church planting team associated with his church. I was curious about this man, such an anomaly, a Turkish convert from Islam now a pastor, and prayed that I could meet him. I wanted to tell him what had happened to the Armenian people, see his response to the horrible crimes against humanity committed by his country and people, but also see what common ground we had in Christ.

One morning all the pastors were invited to take communion at the conference. The Turkish pastor was serving communion directly in front of me. I went to him after the service and explained how my grandfather, Rev. Hovhannes Eskijian had served his people in Aleppo, that he perished during the Armenian Genocide, the unfolding tragedy that he and others, tried to alleviate, that my family knew of many people who had died or whose lives were disrupted by this horrific event. Unexpectedly, I began to weep. At that point the pastor did what the prophets of old did in scripture, he repented with a true heart on behalf of the Turkish people, standing in the gap, and he did, as a brother in Christ would do, embraced me in his arms.

Perhaps such a unique event many years after the Genocide is a foretaste of the only way, I believe, there will be conclusion of this sad and terrible history, a God conclusion, not a man conclusion. As all Armenians, I personally feel grief and anger, and want to see admission of guilt by the Turkish government, justice and restitution on earth. I have no right to forgive on behalf of those who perished and suffered. But by standing in the gap as a Christian, I can take the cross to this bloody territory, and know that trespasses and crimes can only be resolved by the blood of Jesus, generational pain and trauma only healed by the Great Comforter, the Holy Spirit, and restoration only gained through the eternal declaration "it is finished" which Jesus cried in His agony. Someday God will settle all scores on earth at the great white throne judgment, and someday He promises to wipe away all tears—no looking back. Right now it is our job to pray for and assist our brothers and sisters. I think this is how Rev. Eskijian would have viewed it.

Nancy Eskijian, on behalf of the Eskijian Family, April 2015.

The Ararat-Eskijian Museum founded by Mr. Luther Eskijian, now deceased, operates in collaboration with the Genocide Museum-Institute in Erevan, Republic of Armenia. www.ararat-eskijian-museum.com.

Preface by Luther Eskijian

It is impossible that anyone, including myself, could write a proper preface to a book regarding the 1915 Genocide of the Armenian people, and the role that many played in helping to save lives at that desperate time. However, I am privileged to say a few words about my father, Reverend Hovhannes Eskijian who participated in this endeavor.

My mother, Gulenia Danielian Eskijian, knowing the importance of a written historical account of his life and works, collected articles, testimonials, and reports, from the time of his death on March 26th 1916, to her own untimely demise in 1946.

She imparted to me the singular importance of his story, so that it became a lifelong mission.

My father was left an orphan at an early age. His father, Sarkis Eskijian, was a shoemaker in the city of Ourfa, and was brutally murdered by the Turks, when beheaded in the 1895 massacre. I first received information of the manner of my grandfather's death from a native of Ourfa whom I met when I was a young man in the mid-1930s. When this gentleman of about 80 years age heard my name Eskijian connected to the city of Ourfa, he related to me what he knew about the death of my grandfather.

I also learned that my father was placed in an orphanage where he met an American missionary by the name of Corrine Shattuck. In the orphanage my father was introduced to the Christian faith, became deeply committed to the Lord Jesus Christ, and was inspired by Miss Shattuck to become a minister. He attended the Christian American seminary in Marash. In time he met my mother, Gulenia Danielian who was attending the College for Girls in Marash, and they married in 1911.

My father's first church was located in the Kessab area of Syria, where he attended to the spiritual needs of three villages, Ekiz Oluk, Kourkene, and Kaladouran. My brother John and I were born in Ekiz Oluk.

At the end of 1913 my father was called to the Emmanuel church of Aleppo, where he served just as the Armenian nation entered into the heartbreaking events of the Genocide of 1915. The story in the following pages will describe in part how he gave his life to save others, a price he paid in the service of our Lord Jesus Christ. The account of his life is given in the pages of this book as a historical reference of the times, but also, hopefully, as an inspiration to others.

My mother, brother and I came to America in October of 1920, following father's death and the end of the Genocide of our people. In the early days all Armenian newcomers met in church or public events, as we had no radios, televisions, and practically no telephones. So the exchange of information was by direct contact. When people found out that my name was Eskijian they would invariably ask if I was the son of Reverend Eskijian. They would relate how my father had saved their life or a relative's, or how he inspired them in the Christian life and gave them hope in a troubled time by his example. In my youth I was told that I should go into the ministry and continue the unfinished work of my father. While this sounded good, it was not possible. No one could fill his shoes. He was a man called for a time and a place and a season, a Spirit-filled, humble, loving sacrificial man of God.

At the age of 16, I, too, gave my life to Jesus Christ. Although I did not know what my life would be, the Lord was with me in my youth, through the Depression and World War II. Upon my return from Europe and the war, I realized that I could serve the Lord and earn a living at the same time. Even though I had a young family to support, I could also work in my church, teach Sunday school, assist the church with my profession of architecture, all of which developed into nearly full time ministry.

My service to the greater community and the Armenians has included the start of an Armenian museum, the Ararat-Eskijian Museum in Mission Hills, California, designing and building Christian day schools, churches for Armenian, African-American, and American congregations. No, I did not follow my father in the ministry, but I did follow the Lord's will in my life, which is all He asks. This was made possible by the love and support of my wife Anne, at my side at all times, who was devoted to our home and children.

My father's legacy has not ended. Our oldest daughter, Carol Kazanjian, is a mother of three young men, raising them in the nurture and admonition of the Lord with her husband Howard Kazanjian. They will have to overcome the fast pace of the electronic age, with the vision of timeless Christian values.

Our son Martin, is an outstanding engineer, serving the Lord by ministry to the elderly on Sundays, at present, and many other phases of ministry in the past.

Our youngest daughter, Nancy, is an attorney who divides her time between the practice of law and pastoring an inner city store front church with others. The mission of the church is to meet the spiritual needs of the congregation, introducing them to their Savior, Jesus Christ, as well as reach out in tangible ministry of food, clothes, and daily necessities. The conditions in which Nancy ministers are not much different from those of my father. The purpose: To reclaim lives that are lost and floundering by introducing them to the saving knowledge and power of Jesus Christ.

The writing of this book has been a lifelong goal. How it was to be accomplished was not determined until by chance a young energetic German historian crossed my path in 1999. He had been researching the Genocide for many years, including investigation into Turkish and German archives. He came across the name of Reverend Hovhannes Eskijian in several places, never expecting to meet a descendant of the man. But the Lord has many ways to honor His servant. Suddenly last year Hilmar Kaiser found me and the storehouse of information that we had been collecting about my father. Now he could close a chapter on the life of one who lived and died for his people, and I could close a mission in my own life, started decades ago. I am now 87 years old.

Luther Eskijian
April 2001

Editor's note: Luther Eskijian passed away in 2007 and Anne Eskijian passed away in 2010. Carol and Howard Kazanjian's children now have homes of their own; Martin and his wife Effie Eskijian serve the Armenian community; and Nancy Eskijian is in full time ministry in the inner city. The Ararat-Eskijian Museum continues to educate and give a voice to those who survived and those who perished in the Armenian Genocide.

Preface by Hilmar Kaiser

The present study is the result of two independent research projects on the Armenian Genocide. One project is my own, the other is that of a family of Genocide survivors. Over the past ten years, I have spent considerable time and effort in various archives, libraries, and other relevant collections in Europe, the U.S., and the Middle East. My main object was to obtain primary information on the planning, execution, and impact on the victims of the – as far as we know - first administratively organized genocide in history. In the course of my research, I found information on numerous perpetrators, by-standers, and victims. Accounts of resistance against deportations and massacres, aside from the well-known episodes at Van, Ourfa, and a few other places, however, remained very scarce and fragmentary. Nevertheless, some information occasionally came to light. The experiences of a Swiss woman, Beatrice Rohner, attracted my special interest. I tried to reconstruct her activities at Aleppo in 1915-1917. Soon, however, I understood that her work had depended on the efforts of a local Armenian underground network active in the city. The few details I could gather from Ottoman and German sources remained fragmentary but I understood that a Protestant pastor by the name of Eskijian had played a critical role. Later, I found a copy of John Minassian's outstanding memoirs, *Many Hills Yet to Climb,* which gave some deeper insights into Armenian humanitarian resistance in Aleppo, written by one of the very few survivors of that remarkable effort.

In 1999, I participated at an academic conference in Los Angeles. During a break between the sessions, I tried to relax a little outside the conference hall. Suddenly, I heard the word "Eskijian." I was electrified and rushed to the two persons who seemed to speak about Eskijian. To my surprise I learned that a certain Luther Eskijian was living in Altadena and I even got his phone number. I rushed to a friend and colleague of mine, J. Michael Hagopian, and insisted that we call Mr. Eskijian immediately and arrange a meeting the next day. The following day we met in Altadena and after a while Luther Eskijian opened a safe. He took out a large box with material about his father, Hovhannes Eskijian, the Reverend of Aleppo. The collection was the result of Luther Eskijian's decades of dedicated endeavor to learn more about his father and his work. Over the following months, we met several times and put together the information we both had. In the end, Luther Eskijian suggested to produce this volume that would be a first step towards a history of the Armenian underground in Aleppo and also on the work of Reverend Hovhannes Eskijian.

Working on the project, I understood that I would not be able to do full justice to the motives of the Reverend because I lacked the necessary religious training to comprehend some key aspects of his work. To overcome this shortcoming, Nancy Eskijian, the Reverend's grandaughter, added a chapter focusing on the religious aspects of the humanitarian work at Aleppo. In writing these lines, I realize that we still know too little about those outstanding personalities that had the vision for a future after the Genocide. It was their unselfish and tireless struggle that secured the survival of the remnants of the Ottoman Armenian communities. All of them knowingly risked their lives and most of them died in the pursuit of their humanitarian goals. Perhaps this small volume will help their story or at least ensure that a small part of it will not be forgotten.

I am indebted to many people for their support on this project. Among them are the Eskijian family, Ara Sarafian, my friend and colleague, Sirvart Sarafyan who translated Armenian sources for me, Barbara Gillmore and J. Michael Hagopian of the Armenian Film Foundation for helping me during my visits to Los Angeles.

Hilmar Kaiser
Rome, April 2001

Ottoman Empire circa 1915

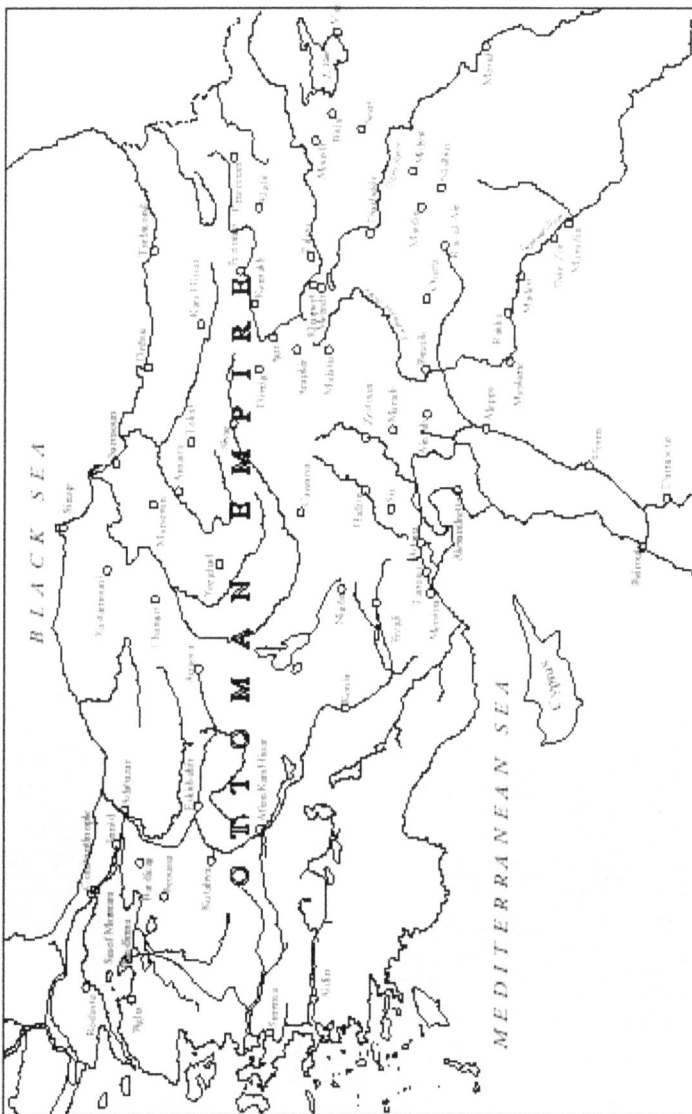

At the Crossroads of Der Zor
1915-1917

Introduction

Now more than one hundred years after the crime, much of the history of the Armenian Genocide remains an untold story.* Some of the gaps in our knowledge are being filled by narrative accounts: more and more survivor memoirs and other documentary publications are becoming available. Meanwhile, although no comprehensive account of the organization and execution of the crime has been published to this day, a growing number of monographic studies have been written in recent years. The present study belongs to the category of narration.

The history of Armenian orphans during the Genocide has been largely neglected in Western-language scholarship. The same holds true for the study of humanitarian resistance against the Ottoman extermination program. Research in both fields is, however, indispensable for an adequate understanding of the nature of the crime. The fate of Armenian orphans demonstrates that the Armenian Genocide was not simply a general massacre but a differentiated program. This program allowed for the forcible assimilation into Muslim communities of clearly identified victims, such as young children and young women. In these individual cases, assimilation served the Ottoman government's purposes more than murder. The central authorities in Constantinople did not, however, plan other important exemptions from the extermination program. Some of the deported Armenians managed to make themselves useful to local authorities and thereby gained a reprieve. Corruption of individual officials and profiteering provided other avenues for survival.

The assimilation or extermination of Armenians was not an erratic process. At Constantinople, officials of the Ottoman Ministry of the Interior acted in a carefully calculated manner and assured, as far as possible, the faithful execution of their orders. Consequently, very little room was left for individual decision making at the local level. Ottoman officials who encountered Armenian deportees on their way to extermination were not supposed to act at their own discretion, but to function as elements of a larger bureau-

---

*   Hilmar Kaiser's original introduction noted "eighty-five" years after the crime. This special edition updates that figure.

1

cratic machine. As we will see, however, many officials did not do this. For a variety of reasons, humanitarian or simply pecuniary, these officials acted in ways that would not merit the approval of the central government. Some of these officials had to face consequences like being removed from their post or even murder.[1]

Another serious obstacle for the Ottoman government presented itself in the form of foreign interference with the extermination program. While it remains true that no decisive intervention on behalf of Ottoman Armenians took place, some aid and assistance arrived in time. Once information on the deportations and massacres became available, philanthropic groups in Europe and the United States organized what was up to that time a unique international relief effort. The relief work brought together diverse groups that had not formerly worked together or assisted each other. Most importantly, this international campaign made a difference in the daily struggle of Armenians for survival. Nevertheless, only a minority of those who received relief actually survived until the defeat of the Ottoman Empire and eventual rescue from a systematic campaign of mass murder. Those who did survive formed the core of new, fragmented communities in exile following World War I.

One of the preconditions that made such a relief effort possible was the support channeled through United States and German government circles. The United States government and particularly the United States embassy at Constantinople sustained the relief effort in every possible way. The German role was somewhat more ambiguous. German government support was the result of a calculus that tried to balance humanitarian concerns with the German government's interest in maintaining good relations with its Ottoman wartime ally, as well as appeasing international public opinion. Nevertheless, German consular officials, military officers, and other individuals did not necessarily share their government's attitude. Missionaries, consuls, and community leaders quickly began to denounce the genocide against Armenians and tried their best to bring about a change of policy. At a more immediate level, these groups organized relief efforts and often acted independently of German government directives.[2]

The relief effort depended first of all on the active role played by Armenian community members. In fact, Armenian communities that had not yet been deported in the summer of 1915, as well as individual deportees themselves, organized the first networks for survival. Since only very few foreigners could actually join the relief effort within the Ottoman provinces, the major load for relief work fell upon the shoulders of those who were earmarked for extermination. These workers accepted the risks associated with their humanitarian efforts against the efforts of the Ottoman government and many paid the highest price for their selfless work. The origins of these relief efforts have been little understood to date.

It is true that abundant and authoritative information exists on the organization of relief work in the United States.[3] The original appeals for help, however, came from the victims themselves. The Armenian organizers of relief networks had a clear vision of what could and had to be done. At one crucial location, the city of Aleppo, the struggle began not simply for the survival of individual deportees, but for what Armenian relief workers understood to be the survival of their whole nation. They engaged in this humanitarian resistance right under the eyes of the Ottoman authorities. In a large city like Aleppo, with plenty of places to hide and a need for cheap labor, opportunities existed that allowed for the creation of underground shelters.

In a fateful decision, Reverend Hovhannes Eskijian, a key player in the struggle, identified the survival of the Armenian orphans in his city and that of the few remaining teachers, physicians, and other intellectuals, as the only way to enable the reemergence of an Armenian community after the Genocide. Thus, the fight for the survival of orphaned children became a main axiom of combating the Ottoman government's genocidal logic. In the final analysis, the success of the humanitarian resistance depended not on the total number of survivors, but on the number of young Armenians who could avoid death or forced assimilation and form new Armenian families.

As in any other case of resistance against a terrorist regime, the activists had to exercise great caution and avoid leaving traces of their activities. Consequently, few testimonies of survivors and even fewer archival records have been preserved attesting to their work. Reverend Eskijian died in March 1916 and did not leave behind private papers. His family, however, collected as much information on his work as possible. Some survivors who knew Eskijian also made a point of expressing their gratitude to him for their survival. One of them, John Minassian, left behind a detailed account of the underground work that was being carried out in 1915. This account provides unique insights into the daily struggle that took place in Aleppo.

When Reverend Eskijian died, his work was continued first by his Armenian collaborators and later by Beatrice Rohner. She was a Swiss missionary in the service of the Deutscher Hülfsbund für christliches Liebeswerk im Orient (German Aid Society for Christian Relief Work in the Orient). As an employee of a German organization and a Swiss citizen, unlike her deceased Armenian partner she enjoyed the protection of German diplomats. She produced a series of reports that were filed with the German Foreign Office and the American Board of Commissioners for Foreign Missions (ABCFM). Her accounts provide insights into the events at Aleppo as they unfolded from 1915 to 1917. While some of the material almost instantly gained critical international importance, her activities and those of her associates have received only limited attention.

This study is based on an array of published sources, as well as German, United States, and Turkish archival collections that contain abundant information on the Armenian GENOCIDE in general, and the events that took place around Aleppo in particular. Some of the sources from the Prime Minister's archives in Turkey are introduced here for the first time.

This study will start with a short overview of the Ottoman war effort leading up to 24 April 1915, the beginning of the Armenian Genocide. Following a brief account of the initial phase of the genocide, the Ottoman deportation policy will be described. As a result of the centrally coordinated deportations, Aleppo turned into a crossroads for the deportees, where in most cases the Ottoman authorities determined their final fate. Drawing primarily on German consular communications, the study will follow the deadly consequences of the deportations.

In response to appeals from Aleppo and other places, United States, German and other missionary circles organized an international relief effort in support of the deportees. Right from the start of the humanitarian work, Ottoman and German policy considerations shaped the work. German missionary circles had to overcome German government opposition before they could join their United States colleagues and establish together an extensive relief network in the fall and winter of 1915.

The international relief effort was, however, not the first aid program organized. Already in summer 1915 Armenian residents of Aleppo had established an effective underground network helping the deportees that passed through the city or stayed there for a while. Reverend Hovhannes Eskijian played a leading role in these endeavors. Based on fragmentary accounts of survivors and some remaining documentation from other sources, the importance of this almost forgotten Armenian community leader will be demonstrated.

The death of Eskijian and the intensified repression of the humanitarian resistance at Aleppo by the Ottoman authorities put an end to Eskijian's underground network. The arrest and murder of Eskijian's team formed part of a general Ottoman roundup of still surviving Armenians in the spring of 1916. In the same manner, the Ottoman government put an end to the attempts of Beatrice Rohner to continue the work among the deportees in the concentration camps of the Syrian desert and her hopes to protect the Armenian orphans that had remained so far under her care. Like aides of Eskijian before, those of Rohner fell victim to the killers of the Ottoman government.

The final chapter gives a cautious assessment of the accomplishments of the humanitarian resistance, underlining the finding of this study that the Ottoman Armenians were the victims of the Ottoman government. They did not, however, give up their struggle for survival and were not passive. On the contrary, they had a clear vision for the future, defying the genocidal program of the Ottoman government.

The Ottoman War Effort in 1914–15

On 2 August 1914 the Ottoman and German governments signed a treaty of alliance. That agreement and further political pressure from Germany secured the Ottoman participation in World War I on the side of the Central Powers. On 29 October 1914 the Ottoman navy attacked Russian ports on the Black Sea coast, thereby leading to a declaration of war by the Entente powers. Germany and Austria-Hungary welcomed the Ottoman attack very much, as their campaigns against Russia and the war on the western front had entered a critical military phase. The Ottoman army concentrated a large part of its troops close to Constantinople and the straits, while the Ottoman Third Army (and troops of what would become later the Ottoman Fourth Army) began preparations to attack the Suez Canal and the Transcaucasian provinces of the Russian empire. A supporting attack was also planned against neutral Persia, while only minor forces were left behind in Iraq. The plans were ambitious and depended on taking the enemy forces by surprise. The Ottoman army had not recovered from its crushing defeat in the Balkans Wars of 1912–13 and badly needed trained officers as well as supplies of all kinds. While a defensive strategy could have generated favorable results by taking advantage of the mountainous and desert terrain in the border regions, Enver Pasha, the Ottoman minister of war, miscalculated the relative strength of his forces and entertained dreams of conquests.

Eskijian family photograph (Ekizoluk, Kessab, cir. 1913)

The Ottoman attacks failed miserably. By February 1915 the Russians had effectively destroyed the Ottoman Third Army. In Persia, Ottoman troops were able to occupy Tabriz for a short while, but they soon had to flee. In Iraq, British troops advanced on Baghdad after having routed an Ottoman force. In Egypt, the British repulsed the Ottoman attack on the Suez Canal and began preparations for an attack on Palestine.[4] Now, the initiative passed on to the Entente. Britain and France began to assemble a major fleet at the Dardanelles in what could only be understood as an attempt to seize the straits and the Ottoman capital. Although the Ottoman army had concentrated reinforcements in the area, the general outlook for the Ottoman war effort seemed to turn from bad to worse. In early 1915 the coastal defenses at the Dardanelles were under the command of the German admiral Guido von Usedom, who gave a sober assessment of the military situation. He stated that he could guarantee that he would be able to hold his positions against a first attack, but was unable to give the same assurance in case of a second attempt by the Entente.[5]

The defenders indeed managed to repulse the first naval attack, but in March the Ottoman government panicked and prepared the evacuation of the imperial court and its administration to inland provinces. The situation in the eastern provinces also deteriorated and Ottoman forces and administrators turned on the local Armenian population by looting and killing. The outrages in the area around Lake Van culminated into a full-fledged campaign against the Armenians by the middle of April. In the city of Van, the provincial capital, the Armenian population saw no other way to avoid massacre than to organize a resistance against the Ottoman army by barricading itself in the Armenian town quarter.[6] In other areas of the empire, Armenians and other Christian Ottoman soldiers serving in the Ottoman army were disarmed and put into labor battalions. By April Ottoman military authorities considered evacuating Armenian villages close to supply lines in Cilicia and northern Syria.

A militarily insignificant clash between some Armenian deserters and bandits and Ottoman security forces close to the mountain town of Zeitoun was given critical importance. The place was predominantly inhabited by Armenians who had a history of active resistance against attacks on the part of Muslim marauders. The Ottoman army immediately mobilized far superior forces against several dozen Armenians who had barricaded themselves near the city. When the reinforcements arrived at Zeitoun, the whole affair was already practically over. Several deserters and gendarmes had been killed during a short skirmish. The surviving deserters had taken to the mountains and were out of reach. Djemal Pasha, the commander of the Ottoman Fourth Army, decided, however, to use the episode to preempt all potential future trouble with Armenians at Zeitoun. He ordered the deportation of the population. On 26 March 1915 he informed the Ministry of the Interior that the deportees would be sent to the province of Konya. The men and older boys, however, were sent to Der Zor.[7]

The Start of the Armenian Genocide

The attitude of the ruling dictatorial regime in Constantinople, the Committee for Union and Progress, toward its Armenian citizens grew increasingly hostile. In Constantinople Armenian leaders worked hard to assure the government of Armenian loyalty but to no avail. On 24 April 1915 the Ottoman government ordered the arrest of several hundred Armenian leaders in Constantinople and many more in the provinces. The victims were caught by surprise and almost no one escaped the roundup. Those arrested were quickly sent to inland destinations where they were later killed. Very few survived and were later released.[8] On the same day, Talaat Bey, the minister of the interior, ordered that those deportees from Zeitoun who were still on their way to Konya province should be sent to the Syrian desert district of Der Zor. The Ottoman authorities wanted to avoid concentrations of Armenians in the province of Konya. At the same time the inhabitants of Armenian villages close to the Mediterranean littoral and several mountain towns and hamlets, some of which were situated close to supply routes, were deported from the Adana province.[9]

The effective liquidation of the community leadership rendered the Armenian community unable to offer any organized resistance against what was ahead. On 24 May 1915 the Entente published a declaration in which the powers announced that they would hold personally responsible all Ottoman civilians and officials who were implicated in atrocities against Armenians.[10] The psychological effect on the Ottoman leaders was tremendous. In haste the Ottoman Council of Ministers passed a "provisional law" that was intended as a legal cover for a general deportation of the empire's Armenian population. A series of administrative manuals provided guidelines to the provincial and local authorities in regard to Armenian property and the scheduling of the deportations. The central authorities ordered deportations for various districts and oversaw the progress of the deportees on their way to the Syrian desert, the final destination for the victims.[11]

The fate of the deportees varied considerably according to their region of origin. Armenians living in the western provinces had a comparably good chance of survival to Aleppo. Most of them were deported by railway or were marched along the railroad tracks. These deportees were not subjected to large-scale massacres like their counterparts in the eastern provinces.[12] The conditions were, nevertheless, atrocious. One of the deportees was Elise Hagobian Taft. Until the summer of 1915, the little girl had lived with her family in the town of Bandirma. Late in August of that year, the Ottoman authorities deported the whole Armenian population of this coastal town located on the shores of the Marmara Sea. While the deportees were not forced to walk the whole distance to Aleppo, railway transportation was by no means a humane way of deporting the victims:

> It was August and hot. The box cars were suffocating as the sun beat down on them. We had no water; sanitary facilities were frightful. Just a pile of straw at each end of our boxer—one each for the men and the women—and the stench was overpowering in the cramped quar-

ters. Whenever the train stopped we could push back the side doors and rush out—the men on one side, the women on the other—and use the fields for latrines. The soldiers would round us back with curses and the butts of rifles, and slam the door shut. Infants cried, trying to suckle on drying breasts. They wetted and dirtied themselves, adding to the stench. There were pregnant women, some in advanced stages and the Lord only knows how they fared.

　　　The men seemed helpless. Used to the outdoors, this cramped cattle car with the suffering wives, children and kin was not their world. They were confused, unnerved, pathetic to watch in their inability to take charge or to comfort their families as they had taken pride in doing all their lives. The women proved more resourceful and adaptable, and made do with the situation at hand. They put together what there was of bread and food and fed the children and husbands. And it was the women who kept up morale by singing Der Voghormya ("Lord Be Merciful") a religious chant.[13]

The railway stations of the Anatolian and Baghdad railway lines and nearby fields had turned into concentration camps where tens of thousands of deportees were kept, waiting to be dispatched toward the Syrian desert. As these camps lacked even minimal infrastructure, such as sanitary installations, the deportees began to organize rudimentary communal structures for the duration of their stay at these places. The principal goal was to render conditions as bearable as possible—an almost impossible endeavor under the given conditions. At Afyon, a city along the railway line north of Konya, the younger members of Armenian communities had taken the lead:

　　　Brother Garo with a few other energetic Armenian youths formed a "police force" for sanitary purposes; they watched the deportees closely so that people would not relieve themselves close to the camp. I remember how an old man from our hometown broke the "law" and my brother caught him at it. The old man pleaded that "it was only a drop" and my brother answered, "Why didn't you drink it if it was only a drop?" This camp of exiles was an endless sight and it extended beyond eyes' reach. There were so many different Armenians with different dialects.[14]

The help that deportees received from outside sources was very limited and inadequate in view of the distress. About fifty thousand deportees camped near the Konya railway station in open fields without any shelter. Starving deportees sold young girls to Muslims for 20 piastres in order to obtain some bread. The competition for the few relief funds was fierce. Soon Catholic Armenian deportees blamed Protestant missionaries of discriminating against Catholics. Many Catholic deportees felt deserted by their church and began to reassess their religious allegiance. In despair, Catholic priests im-

plored the Armenian Catholic patriarchate in Constantinople to send more
funds and intervene with United States ambassador Henry Morgenthau. The
apostolic delegate to Constantinople, Monsignor Angelo Maria Dolci, approached Morgenthau. The diplomat promised to ensure the equal distribution of funds. Dolci, however, remained skeptical. Suspected discrimination
remained an issue throughout 1915 and 1916. Some Catholic priests even
suggested that the relief effort should be separated according to religious
affiliation. This way, the Catholic clergy would gain full control of funds
due to deported Armenian Catholics. There is evidence that deportees knew
some of the mechanics of the ongoing relief effort. They used their own
church hierarchy to lobby for redistribution of funds. The deportees were
not just passive recipients of charity but tried to mould relief efforts according to their own views and interests.[15]

The treatment of Armenians in eastern Asia Minor was decidedly more
atrocious. In areas where a Russian intervention was theoretically possibly,
the army massacred the local Armenians in their settlements or nearby.[16] In
regions further removed from the front lines, the deportations began often
with the separation of the men and older boys from their families. While
the women and children were sent off to the desert, the men and boys were
killed at a short distance from their homes at a remote location. On their way
to the desert, women and children were sometimes subjected to a series of
massacres. The killings dramatically reduced the number of the deportees.
Those who survived the march through the mountains met with the deportees from the western provinces near Aleppo or close to the Baghdad Railway line in northern Syria.[17]

By June 1915 Aleppo became a crossroads where the fate of deportees
was decided. During the first months of the Armenian Genocide, those deportees who were lucky were sent south to areas in the Hauran or towns like
Hama, Homs, and Kerek. Many deportees managed to remain in Damascus
or made their way to Jerusalem. The majority of deportees, however, were
sent southeast from Aleppo and the railway line into the Syrian desert. Here
the Ottoman authorities organized a network of concentration camps along
the Euphrates toward the town of Der Zor and beyond.[18] In the concentration camps the Ottoman authorities systematically exposed the deportees
to starvation, dehydration, and contagious diseases like typhus. The diseases
particularly claimed many victims among the weakened Armenians. Mass
graves and unburied corpses lined the road along the Euphrates for hundreds of miles.[19]

Aleppo during the First Months of the Armenian Genocide

Aleppo was the commercial center for northern Syria. It was where the Syrian French railway network and the German Baghdad Railway met. The critical importance of Aleppo for military provisioning was underlined by the establishment of a German military transportation center that coordinated the traffic to the front lines in Arabia and the eastern provinces. Moreover, Aleppo was where the Baghdad Railway company maintained a directorate for the construction of its line in northern Mesopotamia.[20] Given the importance of the city, Germany, Austria-Hungary, and the United States maintained consulates in Aleppo. While the Austro-Hungarian consul hardly reported on the Genocide, his German and United States colleagues filed numerous reports as part of their job. United States consul Jesse A. Jackson and German consul Walter Rössler went far beyond the call of their official duties.

On 12 March 1915 Rössler reported to the German embassy that a revolt had broken out in Zeitoun, a small mountain town mostly inhabited by Armenians. The German missionary Karl Blank had informed the consulate and asked for the consul's intervention.[21] Rössler wanted to intervene and avoid disturbances but was stopped by the embassy on the initiative of a German officer serving in the Ottoman army.[22] The affair had some impact on Rössler. In the coming months, he would carefully guard his sources of information and only occasionally reveal the identity of his informants. For the time being, he worked with the governor of Aleppo, Djelal Bey, to mitigate the central government's orders that were directed against Armenians. Meanwhile, United States consul Jackson supplied his government such information as he could gather. His assessment was similar to that of his German colleague. On 5 June, only three months after the Zeitoun affair, Jackson could sum up his views stating: "It is without doubt a carefully planned scheme to thoroughly extinguish the Armenian race."[23]

By that date, the central government had sent Ahmed Eyoub Bey to Aleppo. The official belonged to the Ottoman Ministry of the Interior's "Directorate for the Settlement of Tribes and Immigrants" (IAMM). This department was charged with the execution of the deportations and had subdepartments in all major provinces and subprovinces. Eyoub Bey became the director of the subdepartment at Aleppo and was therefore responsible for the deportations in the province.[24] Rössler concluded that Eyoub's appointment effectively obstructed Djelal's efforts on behalf of the Armenians. To offset the impact of the newly arrived official's activities, Rössler suggested that the German embassy should intervene with the Ottoman government. The consul explained that Armenians had been deported for security reasons. The Ottoman military suspected that they could pose a threat in case of a landing of Entente troops on the coast. In Aleppo, however, these reasons were no longer valid. Rössler argued that the Armenians should be allowed to remain in the city and the surrounding districts. He reported that Armenian deportees were dispersed in small groups among Arab villages in the steppes east of the town. Many deportees had died because of deprivations and excesses. Women were raped, and especially the old and very young did not survive for long.[25] Rössler also forwarded an appeal by the catholicos of Sis to the Armenian patriarchate at Constantinople. The document confirmed in detail the previous urgent messages of the German consul.[26]

On 21 June 1915 Rössler informed his superiors that Djelal Bey's resistance against the deportation of Armenians from Aleppo was about to lead to his removal. The Ottoman government had ordered him to exchange his post with that of the governor of Angora. The change did not promise anything good for Armenians. On the same day, Rössler reported that the governor of Diarbekir, Dr. Reshid Bey, had persecuted the Armenians there with special severity. Gendarmes had killed Armenian men wholesale. Djelal Bey had shared his strong resentment against Reshid Bey's activities and counteracted some government orders.[27]

By the end of the month, Rössler had lost all trust in the good faith of the Ottoman government. Two well-known Armenian members of the Ottoman parliament, Zohrab and Vartkes Effendis, were deported from Constantinople to Diarbekir via Aleppo. They were supposed to face charges in an Ottoman court martial. Rössler suspected that the two would be assassinated on the road east of Aleppo. Weeks later he had to report that his apprehensions had been justified. By the beginning of July, Aleppo had become a center for information on the atrocities in the eastern provinces of the empire. German officers, engineers, and other travelers reported on their experiences. Gendarmes had burned down Armenian villages and massacred the inhabitants. Corpses tied together floated down the Euphrates. An Ottoman district governor had been murdered when he refused to carry out massacres ordered by the government. At the same time, more and more deportees arrived in Aleppo before they were sent on to their final destination. Many women had left their small children behind in the town, hidden under blankets. This way, they hoped, at least their children would survive the deportations and avoid being massacred.[28]

The removal of Djelal Bey seemed to have opened the way for the deportation of the inhabitants of Armenian villages in the surrounding districts of Aleppo. Rössler implored the embassy and the Foreign Office to do all in their power to prevent or at least mitigate these deportations. He added once more a long list of recent massacres and emphasized the Ottoman authorities' responsibility for and participation in the killings. Rössler also advised the German government that it should not disseminate Ottoman propaganda that denied the extermination of the Armenians. Rössler reported that by the end of July, 15,328 had arrived in the desert city of Der Zor. About ten thousand had remained in the city, while the others were kept in the surrounding countryside. These were the Armenians who had been the first deportees sent from the Cilician districts. In Aleppo itself, fourteen thousand deportees had arrived; ten thousand of them had remained there. Rössler stressed that these deportees had fared much better than those from the eastern provinces. It appeared that Armenians were just beginning to arrive in the Aleppo region. More importantly, the authorities kept detailed counts of deportees. The arrivals had to survive in extreme poverty, and soon young girls were traded in the streets.[29]

Although the Ottoman authorities were concerned that news of the ongoing extermination would reach the outside world, it was impossible to hide the disastrous conditions and the human losses inflicted on Armenians. The local Ottoman authorities suspected that Consul Jackson had shared his knowledge with others. Being a consul of a neutral and powerful state, Jackson was relatively safe. Thus, the only thing the local authorities could do was to intimidate him. Jackson, however, continued like Rössler to report on what he had seen and learned.[30] Some of Jackson's information came from two Armenian volunteer relief workers who had reached the concentration camps. Reverend Sahag and the pharmacist Sarkis had traveled to Der Zor and distributed money. Their work had, however, attracted the attention of the provincial authorities at Aleppo who informed Talaat. The Ministry of Interior gave strict orders to ascertain how the two men had been able to travel so far and "secretly" distribute money. Two days later Talaat ordered the officials at Der Zor to apprehend the two men and send them back to Aleppo.[31]

The appalling conditions prompted the German consul to renew his appeals to his superiors to try their best to prevent the deportation of more Armenians. In August Rössler estimated that about forty thousand Armenians had already been deported from the western provinces alone and he feared that this number would rise to 150,000 once the deportations were extended to other parts of the western provinces as well. Unless foreign relief became available to the victims, Rössler expected thousands to die in the coming months. Meanwhile the authorities in Aleppo had already received orders concerning the deportation of Armenian women, children, and young boys and girls under the age of seventeen. These instructions came at a time when Rössler feared that the systematic massacre of deportees had been extended from the eastern provinces to his consular district as well. Djelal Bey's successor, Bekir Sami Bey, pledged to prevent such atrocities, but even the usual deportations constantly claimed many lives, as the deportees were left without the necessary supplies.[32]

By the middle of August, the empirewide deportations had made a strong impact on the local Ottoman administration. The arriving deportees were treated differently according to their places of origin. Cilician Armenians received limited assistance from the local authorities at irregular intervals, while those who had survived the death marches from the eastern provinces received nothing. Six thousand deportees were left in Aleppo with no means of survival and every day about three hundred more arrived. The local Armenian community did its best to feed them, but the funds were quickly exhausted. Rössler forwarded the community's urgent appeals for help from American and German missionary circles.[33]

Rössler's hopes to stop the expected new deportations in his district were frustrated when the Ottoman authorities began deporting the Armenians of Marash. The consul tried his best to protect the Armenian personnel of German missionary institutions but failed. German protection only covered the European staff of the missionary institutions, though Rössler managed to secure the support of the embassy for his own Armenian staff. As a result of this intervention, the Ottoman authorities exempted the consulate employees from deportation. At Aleppo, the consul succeeded in obtaining from the governor an unofficial one-week delay in the deportation of Protestant Armenians.[34] The intensified deportations had brought so many deportees to Aleppo that the local administration had steadily lost control and supervision over the number of Armenians in the city. Thus, officials changed their policy and made more use of railway transport. Now, Armenians were not allowed, as far as possible, to remain in Aleppo pending further deportations. Instead, deportees were forced to camp at some distance from the city along the rail tracks. As a result, new concentration camps emerged for deportees in transit.

An Entrance to Hell: The Concentration Camp of Katma

The most infamous of these new transit camps was situated close to the small railway station of Katma. The misery of the survivors and daily death toll among deportees arriving from the western provinces surpassed most of what they had gone through so far.

Vahram Daderian was a young boy of fifteen years when his family was deported from the town of Tchorum in northern Asia Minor. The father had been a well-to-do businessperson who had organized the Armenian benevolent union of his town. Having been deported on 29 July, the family arrived at Katma on 6 September 1915. In comparison to other deportees, the Daderians had been rather fortunate thus far. They could afford better transport, owned a horse, and still had some other possessions like tents and cooking utensils with them. Vahram kept a diary and recorded the events as they unfolded. On Katma he wrote:

> We finally arrived at Gatma, whose name for many days we already knew. This is the gate to Aleppo. Where all the Turkish caravans are headed. And because they don't want Aleppo to be overcrowded and famine stricken, every day groups of refugee caravans are arriving here. The government has established a refugee center, in order to arrange for their travel away from Aleppo to the endless deserts. But every day when 10 families are leaving tomorrow one thousand arrive. For this reason the Gatma refugee center, after filling up, has expanded into the horizon, covering the whole area with a blanket of colorful tents. The sea of people with coaches, horses, donkeys, mules and people are filled in all direction. The atmosphere is filled with a deafening sound of cursing, crying, and sighing. Skeleton arms are stretched out every where, asking for a piece of bread. As we more forward, we feel that we get deeper in the blood and tears, pain and suffering an endless sea of humanity.
>
> There is a terrible stink that tears every one's nose. Everywhere is [?] covered with unburned, rotten human waste, corpses etc. Besides that, ten thousand people have left their filth, and have contaminated the whole area, and it is not possible not to choke. Holding our nose and covering our eyes, we proceeded among these corpses and garbage, and after a while we stopped at a place at the end of the tent city, which was specially prepared for us.
>
> The policemen[35] advised us, that our journey has ended, and we can stay there as long as we wish. Up to here, in travelling, we were begging the policemen, that they will give us one or two days' rest, so that we could get rest. Now it is just the opposite, we were asking them not to leave us here. But that was useless. They had done their responsibility. They left us to our fate, and went to bring newer and newer caravans and lead them to this hell. Obligated, we got down from the coaches and realizing that for days we may have to stay there,

we started building our tents. Now we don't smell the stink, our noses fortunately have become insensitive. But the flies are unbearable out here, they are so plentiful, as if the Tarsus parasites. They were coming down on us, like black clouds, and were biting our bodies' open areas with their sting with sharp bites, and we cannot possibly last here. Continually, we move our hands to chase them away, but which one? With thousands sitting on our food and clothing, they are so stubborn and shameless. Even if they die, they won't leave their place. At night when we lit the light in the tent, we caught our breath a little. All the flies, run to the lamp, as if they covered it with a black vale. We got relieved from the problem of the flies, and we went close to the stream, got washed, and got cleaned up. We brought the water with pots, and for the first time, we made fire and cooked a hotmeal.

However, the night was terrible, for toilet we had to go further away, outside of the tent, but wherever we went, it was difficult to find a place to step. When we were advancing in the field, suddenly we felt an open hole in front of our feet. Although it was dark, we could see a dead man in the bottom of the hole. Fearfully screaming, we were running back. And now in front of us there was another hole, and another dead corpse in it. And like this, in every side holes and the unburied dead—men, women, elderly and children. All of them were bare and without clothing, some laying on their faces, and some on their back, or their side.[36]

The next day Vahram walked around the camp and noticed that the deportees were trying to maintain some community life. A church service, attended by hundreds of deportees, had been organized. Close to the railway station, some deportees had established a market, selling goods they had bought outside the camp with the permission of the guards. Everywhere people were dying of diseases. Deported priests and other deportees tried to bury these victims in as dignified a manner as possible. The high social status of the Daderian family became apparent to other deportees at the camp when the catholicos of Cilicia, Sahag II, visited their tent. Finally, some bribes and the father's good connections allowed the family to leave the camp for Aleppo.[37]

Elise Hagobian Taft had arrived at Katma late in December 1915, four months after her family had left Bandirma. She described the scenes she had to witness at Katma in shocking detail:

After the rains finally stopped, father and I left our tent in search of drinking water. The sight before me was horrible beyond description. Hundreds and hundreds of swollen bodies lay in the mud and puddles of rain water, some half-buried, others floating eerily in rancid pools, together with rotted bodies and heaps of human refuse accumulated during the week-long rain. Some victims—only the upper torsos emerging from the mud and puddles—were breathing their last. The stench rose to the heavens. It was nauseating beyond belief. The scene was like a huge cesspool laid bare and made to stink even more under a hot sun.

> Just being there made me sick, and I asked father to take me back to our tent. There was no chance of finding safe drinking water anyway. Any water in the area would have been contaminated. It was the ideal breeding ground for the incubation of typhus, typhoid, cholera, smallpox, dysentery and other scourges resulting from such unsanitary conditions.[38]

Naomie Ouzounian of Hadjin was a young girl of fifteen years. She had come back to Hadjin on summer vacation from Constantinople where she attended a boarding school. Her plans for the future had been to become a schoolteacher. Sixty-seven years after her arrival at Katma, she still remembered the place vividly:

> The "camp" where hundreds of thousands had already been thrown together was a narrow strip of the desert, surrounded by bare hills. The hot, humid air was filled with the stench of human refuse and decaying unburied bodies. I couldn't breath, oh, if I could only take a deep breath! The name of this hell was Ghatma. "Dear Lord, I hope there is no Ghatma in the hereafter, and if there is one, forgive my sins and do not condemn me to it," I prayed.[39]

The Ottoman authorities deported the Armenian population of Marash in several waves relatively late in 1915 and in the spring of 1916. Comparatively many deportees from Marash survived and left their testimonies on their experiences at Katma. Some of the deportees had to stay for months at that place. A few managed to make their way out of the unbearable situation by bribing the local officials.[40] Elmasd Santoorian, who later worked as a nurse in Aleppo, confirmed the high death toll among the victims. "I did not witness any killings at Ghatma, probably because the people were dying off faster from disease, starvation, and exposure than their corpses could be carted away on the few donkey-drawn carts available. The most rampant and dreaded diseases were typhus and dysentery. Lice and vermin were everywhere. Ghatma may have looked like Hell itself, but actually it was only its antechamber."[41] Nazareth Yacoobian wrote: "The bulk of the deportees at that place were mostly women and children, for the menfolk had been scythed down on their way southward, especially those hailing from the eastern provinces.... It was not before we reached Ghatma that we realized what the Turks had in store for us. From the very moment that the truth came to all of us, I had only one thought—to flee, to escape."[42]

In November 1915 the German general Colmar Von der Goltz, who had become commander of the Ottoman troops in Iraq, passed through Katma.

A young Armenian student from Zeitoun, Khoren A. Davidson, described later in his life the scene the general observed:

> Katma was a sea of tents. Thousands from Asia Minor were there. Some had been very wealthy at home, but here their present living quarters was a tent fashioned of bed linen or sheets. The four corners of the sheet were tied by string to four wooden pegs in the ground. The sheet was stretched over a wooden rod supported at the ends by two poles. Here was the tent, unprotected from rain, mud, or wind. Eventually, typhus and diarrhoea attacked. People were dying.
>
> We heard it rumored that the idol of Turkey, the German, Von Der Goltz, would come to Katma for a visit. The priest and several others planned to see him and ask for mercy and some Arabian tents. The pasha did not approach the camp. From a distance of two miles, where he stopped his automobile, he viewed the camp through his field glasses. The priest and his company could not approach him. Through his interpreter, the pasha sent word, telling the people not to come close with their typhus germs. Through the interpreter again, the people put their petition before the pasha. He told them that when he was in Aleppo, he would see that those tents they asked for would be sent to them.
>
> He went, but no tents arrived. Instead, there came an edict from him ordering those who could walk to get ready to leave the camp. Those unable to leave would be shot, to end their sufferings in that concentration camp.[43]

Aleppo in the Fall of 1915

By September reports of a cholera epidemic among the twenty thousand deportees interned at Katma reached Aleppo. Every day the authorities filled four trains with deportees and sent them off to Aleppo. The trains remained for several hours at the station and were then sent south toward Damascus. The Armenians were not allowed to leave the railway cars and were heavily guarded in order to prevent them from entering the city. Additionally, each week three trains were filled with deportees who had arrived at Aleppo from the eastern provinces; they were sent south as well. The newly arrived Catholic and Protestant Armenians in the city had enjoyed some protection; now they too were sent on. Only those Protestants and Catholics were allowed to remain in Aleppo who had been registered before the war. The trains had about thirty to thirty-five cars and transported about 1,500 to 1,600 persons, mostly in closed transport cars. Rössler described the scenes at the railway station as "indescribable misery."[44]

Meanwhile a typhus epidemic had broken out in Aleppo. The daily death toll rose from twenty-five to forty, and then to sixty. Most of the victims died of typhus. Understanding that humanitarian appeals alone might be insufficient to generate German support, Rössler pointed out that the military supply lines were threatened by the epidemic. As a result, German soldiers were threatened as well. According to the consul, the only way to reduce the risks was to assist the Armenian deportees medically. As starvation likewise increased, Rössler also asked for more relief funds for the local Armenian community and for the Armenian patriarchate. The lack of food of any kind made death a certain fate for the deportees. Having explained this to his superiors, Rössler suggested that the German embassy should try obtaining renewed exemption for Catholics and Protestants. Clearly, the consul did not give up his attempts to save as many of the deportees as possible. The situation grew continually worse and more desperate. More caravans of women and children arrived from the eastern provinces only to be sent on if they did not die right away in the city. More deportees were sent eastward into the desert to Der Zor. Rössler summarized the authorities' policy that "against the assurances of the Sublime Porte to the contrary, all comes down to the destruction of the Armenian people." Ridiculing official Ottoman propaganda, he asked: "Does the Sublime Porte consider the continued shipment of sick people and children as a political and military necessity?"[45]

On 10 and 12 September, Rössler observed scenes in the streets of Aleppo that impressed him deeply. On both days gendarmes drove about two thousand Armenian women and children through the city, whipping the exhausted deportees on their way toward the railway station. The authorities not only denied the emaciated people water and bread, but they even prevented the local population from distributing water and food. Two women gave birth in the streets and only the intervention of local women saved them from being whipped. The gendarmes, however, dragged another woman along tearing out her hair. Local Germans, and also some Ottoman officers, protested against the atrocious behavior of the gendarmes. At the railway station, even dying people were pushed into the railway cars. Two corpses remained behind. By that time, the daily death toll in Aleppo had increased to at least eighty, while on 26 September, 110 died. A special service collected the dead deportees every day from the streets and buried them in mass graves. At times people who were still alive were buried together with the dead.[46]

Rössler was well informed of the Armenian community's relief efforts. For example, on 23 September 1915, 369 deportees had arrived from forty-three different places and lived in one shelter. Of these 43 were widows, 48 were boys who still had a mother, 132 were boys who had lost both parents, 46 were girls with a mother still living, and 100 were girls who had lost both

parents.[47] Close to the German school in Aleppo, an old inn had been transformed into a refuge for Armenians to die. The students and teachers could
observe how people died lying in the open in their own excrement. Among
orphans who were still alive, the body of another child was putrefying. Martin Niepage, one of the teachers, wrote:

> Opposite the German Technical School at Aleppo, in which we are
> engaged in teaching, a mass of about four hundred emaciated forms,
> the remnant of such convoys, is lying in one of the hans. There are
> about a hundred children (boys and girls) among them, from five
> to seven years old. Most of them are suffering from typhoid and dys-
> entery. When one enters the yard, one has the impression of enter-
> ing a mad-house. If one brings them food, one notices that they
> have forgotten how to eat. Their stomach, weakened by months of
> starvation, can no longer assimilate nourishment. If one gives them
> bread, they put it aside indifferently. They just lie there quietly, waiting
> for death.[48]

In October the situation deteriorated even more. On 17 October 1915 the
authorities ordered further deportation of all Armenians who had illegally
remained in the city. German vice-consul Hoffmann estimated that about
twenty thousand persons were threatened by the order. The deportees were
first to be concentrated in the camps close to the city. During an interview
with the director of the political department of the provincial administration, Hoffmann had learned that about forty thousand Armenians had been
assembled in the concentration camps at Katma and Radju. More were on
their way from the interior provinces and about three hundred thousand
would be transported to "settlement areas" where all would die for want of
supplies and equipment. Instead of providing implements, Ottoman administrators took away all useful implements from the deportees. As immediate
countermeasures, Hoffmann suggested an extensive aid program, the preven-
tion of further deportations, and the possibility for Armenians to emigrate
from the Ottoman Empire. At the same time he tried to save a small group
of families that could claim connections to the German consular service in
one way or another. Likewise, he tried to uphold an exemption from deportation for Protestant and Catholic Armenians. His attempts remained, however, without success.[49] The Ottoman authorities also ordered the catholicos of
Cilicia, who had been in Aleppo since the early summer, to leave the city. He
was supposed to proceed to a Circassian village, Membdj, an infamous place
and the location of a concentration camp on the way to Der Zor.[50]

In November the typhus epidemic continued posing a threat to Ottoman
troops in the area, as well as those passing through Aleppo. Every day about

150 people died of the disease. Djemal Pasha and his staff observed the impact of the epidemic as they moved to the city. Major Dagobert von Mikusch similarly reported the dangers of the epidemic to Fritz Bronsart von Schellendorff, one of the two deputy commanders of the Ottoman General Staff, directly through the German consulate. Friedrich Kress von Kressenstein, a leading German commander in Djemal Pasha's staff, also informed the German admiral Souchon at Constantinople. He stressed that the supply routes were completely contaminated because of the continued deportation of Armenians. Djemal urgently requested the dispatch of a German epidemiologist. Given the urgency of the situation, Djemal also agreed to a proposal that the well-known local physician Dr. Altounian could run a hospital for Armenian deportees.[51]

On 8 November 1915 Consul Rössler submitted a lengthy report to the Foreign Office. He summarized the extermination of the Armenians during the preceding months. Rössler described in detail the scenes he had personally observed on overland routes and within the city itself. The numbers of decomposing bodies along the routes had rendered their disposal impossible. The conditions in the concentration camp at Katma were simply "indescribable." The consul reported that Von Kress was behind Djemal Pasha's visit to Aleppo in order to show his superior the local conditions. The local authorities had done their best to hide the extent of the epidemic but did not succeed. On arrival in Aleppo, Djemal Pasha gave a series of orders to contain the epidemic.[52]

Rössler had also instructed Hoffmann to produce a similar report. Hoffmann gave a comprehensive overview detailing different aspects of the massacres in various regions. He had conducted an extensive inquiry into the matter, interviewing numerous eyewitnesses and evaluating their credibility. He emphasized the brutality of the carnage and quoted numerous reports on the rape of women in shocking detail. Ottoman authorities saw to it that daughters of Armenians who worked for the Baghdad Railway construction teams were included in deportations. Hoffmann could only conclude that rape had became an official policy and that the authorities did not even bother to hide this fact. The desolate conditions of the deportees and the typhus epidemic forced the authorities to speed up deportations. Thus, railway transport was reinstituted after it had been given up at the end of September. Now, however, all deportees had to go to Der Zor or Ras-ul-Ain. The transport to the Hauran and other areas in Syria was strictly prohibited. The Baghdad Railway company received orders to deport fifty thousand Ar-

menians from Katma alone to Ras-ul-Ain. Evidently, Djemal Pasha wanted
to rid himself of the deportees as soon as possible. Hoffmann warned that
the deportation would result in the complete extermination of the Armenian
population. At that moment, the deportation to the desert area east of Aleppo was a certain death sentence for any deportee, even without massacre.

The German consulate systematically collected information on the main
deportation routes that were also major supplies lines for troops. By October Hoffmann estimated the Armenian death toll at around six hundred
thousand. He avoided making a clear statement on the role of the central
government, but quoted Eyoub Bey, the director of the local IAMM sub-
division, who had obstructed aid to Armenian orphans, stating: "You still
don't understand what we want; we want to eradicate the Armenian name."
Hoffmann understood this statement as being representative of the Ottoman government's attitudes.[53]

Rössler was more direct in his assessment of the Ottoman government's
policy. He quoted an Ottoman deportation commissar sent from Constantinople stating: "We want an Armenia without Armenians." The consul
stressed that the government agencies intentionally exterminated the deportees. In other cases, the officials called upon the civilian population and
encouraged it to kill the victims. Rössler made it absolutely clear that he saw
in the killings of Armenian men and boys, and the slow death of women and
children only a difference of method and not of intent. Consequently, he denounced strongly Ottoman and German denial of the Genocide and raised
the issue of German responsibility in his correspondence.[54]

The Ottoman Fourth Army's efforts to contain the typhus epidemic created chaos along the railway line. Dead bodies were lying along the tracks and
in wagons. Any quarantine measures were doomed to fail under such circumstances. However, these efforts had also a positive effect. It provided Rössler
with an opportunity to assist some of the Armenian orphans in the city. He
contacted Von Kress and informed him about a so-called Ottoman orphanage. Each day several children died in the house. After a visit, the German
officer told Rössler that the conditions were beyond description. Von Kress
added that for all other atrocities the Ottoman government could make use
of some excuse like military necessity or lack of control over the deportation
process. In the case of the orphans in Aleppo, however, no such excuse
could be imaginable.[55]

Missionaries from Germany and the United States in the Ottoman Empire

The Ottoman government tried to keep its extermination program a secret. Strict censorship and surveillance of foreigners were quite effective in preventing direct communication between the deportees and the outside world. Some foreigners, however, reported on their experiences and observations once they had left the Ottoman Empire. At the same time, underground reports made available to foreign consuls at Aleppo reached the outside world. The testimonies of missionaries of the ABCFM played a particularly important role in alerting the public in neutral and Entente countries.[56] The ABCFM maintained an extensive network of missionary stations and was by far the largest foreign missionary enterprise in the Ottoman Empire. It commanded considerable influence with United States consuls and the ambassador at Constantinople, as well as with the State Department in Washington, D.C.[57] The ABCFM maintained spacious headquarters in Constantinople, the Bible House, where William W. Peet, the treasurer of the organization in Turkey, coordinated the work and served as a lobbyist with the Ottoman government and the United States embassy.[58] The United States missionary institutions were badly hurt by the extermination campaign. Their various colleges lost their Armenian faculty members and most of their students.[59] As the Ottoman authorities deported Protestant Armenian communities together with Apostolic and Catholic Armenians, the ABCFM effectively lost its base in the Ottoman Empire. Nevertheless, the missionaries did not give up and started their own determined effort to save as many deportees as possible through a quickly established relief network.[60] The work depended on existing mission stations where a reduced staff distributed supplies and money to passing deportees. Local United States consuls, who reported regularly on the persecutions, supported the efforts and functioned as bankers keeping and forwarding relief funds from United States donors.[61]

The second-largest Protestant missionary network in the Ottoman Empire was that of the German Orient Mission and the Deutscher Hülfsbund für christliches Liebeswerk im Orient (German Aid Society for Christian Relief in the Orient). Both organizations were products of the German relief efforts that began after the massacres of Ottoman Armenians in 1894–96. Differences between leading personalities over goals and methods produced a series of splits in the organization. By 1915 the Hülfsbund had emerged as the largest German enterprise, with stations in Van, Moush, Kharpert, Marash, and Harounie in Adana province. The political influence of the

German missionary groups was, however, limited. The German government was more interested in good relations with its Ottoman counterpart and favored the interests of German companies over those of missionaries. Thus, most German missionary work took place in opposition to official German Middle East policies.[62] Like the ABCFM, the Hülfsbund attracted workers for its stations from abroad. Young women from Scandinavian countries and many Swiss citizens joined the organization.[63] One of them was Beatrice Rohner who, like her mother and sister, went to Asia Minor to work at the Marash missionary station. There, the local Hülfsbund and ABCFM stations maintained good relations and cooperated in their work. Thus, when in the fall of 1915 the ABCFM needed personnel for the emergency relief efforts south of Marash along the major highway to Aleppo and in the city itself, Peet turned to the Hülfsbund for assistance.

A Travel Permit to Constantinople

The dramatic reports on the massacres and the fate of Armenian women and children had only limited impact on the German government. German chancellor Theobald Von Bethmann Hollweg regarded the extermination of the Ottoman Armenians as an issue over which he would not risk the Ottoman-German alliance during the ongoing war, even if Armenians would "perish."[64] Thus, damage control ranked high among the priorities of German diplomats. Consequently, German missionary and other religious circles formed a constant source of trouble for the German authorities. As these groups had strong ties with the interior Ottoman provinces, they soon learned the truth about the extermination campaign and began to mobilize their members. Readers of journals like *Sonnenaufgang* (Sunrise) and *Der Christliche Orient* (The Christian Orient) soon learned facts about the deportations that fully contradicted official German and Ottoman government propaganda.[65] Individuals like Johannes Lepsius, the director of the German Orient Mission, and Friedrich Schuchardt, the director of the Hülfsbund, tried to travel to the Ottoman Empire in order to influence the course of events on the spot. Lepsius, who had a history of political cooperation with the German Foreign Office, succeeded in traveling to Constantinople and met with Enver Pasha. However, he did not succeed in influencing the latter in favor of the Armenians.[66]

Schuchardt's steps were much less spectacular. Soon after the reports had reached Germany, he wrote to the Foreign Office, inquiring about the rumors and urging intervention on behalf of Armenians. The German embassy responded evasively. It advised the mission director that effective steps on behalf of Ottoman Armenians had to be postponed until the end of the war. Schuchardt, however, did not give up and asked for an interview at the Foreign Office. The Foreign Office did not agree to the meeting, but had to inform the Hülfsbund that the mission station at Moush was about to be closed by the Ottoman authorities. In view of the overall situation, the diplomats asked Schuchardt to submit a list of all employees and institutions of the Hülfsbund in the Ottoman Empire. The missionaries must have understood that the assurances of the Foreign Office could not be taken too seriously. Schuchardt reacted immediately and also contacted the German embassy at Constantinople.[67]

By August 1915 the Hülfsbund had abundant material on hand to gain a well-informed overview of the Ottoman extermination program. Schuchardt again contacted the Foreign Office and wrote that he had to travel to the Middle East in order to secure the future of his organization's work there. In no uncertain terms, he asked for a travel permit and a series of letters of introduction to foreign embassies. In the enclosures to the request, the Foreign Office found five documents, the content of which completely contradicted the earlier assurances given to the Hülfsbund about the situation in the Ottoman Empire. One day after mailing his request, Schuchardt forwarded another collection of documents on the Genocide to Chancellor Bethmann Hollweg. He denounced the policy of the Ottoman government as simple murder and urged the German government to intervene. He also forwarded additional copies of the new material to the Foreign Office. In both letters Schuchardt argued that only a German intervention could save Germany from the responsibility for the atrocities.[68]

Schuchardt's insistence met with some success. State Undersecretary Arthur Zimmermann cabled the acting German ambassador to Constantinople, Ernst von Hohenlohe-Langenburg, inquiring whether a visit of the mission director would be opportune. The embassy responded promptly that a visit would be out of the question. The diplomats saw no chance that Schuchardt could travel beyond Constantinople. Anyhow, the embassy would do what it could to protect the Hülfsbund stations. The Foreign Office confidentially informed Schuchardt on the results during a meeting at Berlin. The latter, however, did not promise to give up his plans to travel to Constantinople, although he had been told that he could not count on any support from the embassy. One day after Schuchardt's return from Berlin, the managing board of the Hülfsbund met in Frankfurt. The board decided that Schuchardt should not only travel to Constantinople but also try to bring relief to those Armenians who were detained in concentration camps in areas close to Ourfa and Aleppo. The following day Schuchardt forwarded a newly received report to the Foreign Office. Once more, he did not hide his resentment against German publications that denounced Armenians. In closing, he added that he would travel to Constantinople to arrange complicated financial matters. A last attempt of the German embassy at Constantinople to discourage the mission director also had no effect. Thus, the Foreign Office's attempts to influence Schuchardt and to dissuade him from visiting Constantinople failed.[69]

Schuchardt continued to assure the Foreign Office of his loyalty but did not miss the opportunity to express his criticism of German propaganda. He lobbied for changing that policy. Moreover, the director carefully emphasized the importance of the Hülfsbund's work for German prestige among the Ottoman Armenians. Arguing that his organization's work had wider positive political implications, he added that various German consuls could vouch for his person. These continued efforts generated some results. Zimmermann wrote again to the German ambassador at Constantinople and asked the diplomat to consider Schuchardt's request once more. The embassy was less than enthusiastic about the project. It advised the Foreign Office that the Sublime Porte would surely not grant a travel permit for the interior provinces. To avoid complications, the embassy even declined further inquiries in the matter. The Foreign Office cabled immediately the negative result to Schuchardt, but added that a visit, at least to Constantinople, was still not out of the question. The move anticipated a letter of Schuchardt in which the missionary announced his intention to travel exclusively to Constantinople. Within one day, the Foreign Office ascertained that Schuchardt could travel to Constantinople on the condition that he would strictly limit his activities to financial matters and avoid any contact with Armenians. The Foreign Office made this an explicit condition, possibly in reaction to a new request from Schuchardt. The director had asked for travel documents for an employee of the Hülfsbund, Beatrice Rohner, who had worked for a long time with Armenians. The moment the Foreign Office's travel permission arrived in Frankfurt, Schuchardt organized his affairs and quickly left for Constantinople.[70]

The change in the Foreign Office's policy was not accidental. The Ottoman efforts to keep the extermination of Armenians secret had failed.

The Swiss and United States missionary associations had launched an international campaign on behalf of Armenians. Moreover, papers in Entente countries had raised the issue of German complicity. Thus, it became increasingly difficult for the Foreign Office to put off Schuchardt's continued requests. The mission director was without doubt cognizant of the wider implications of his demands. He deliberately made it clear that his activities would have a positive impact on the German image abroad. Further refusal to assist Schuchardt could have easily created a whole series of new complications for the Foreign Office. The latter could not ignore the fact that the Hülfsbund had a branch in Switzerland, a neutral state. Therefore, it was not feasible to hope that the Foreign Office's refusal would go unnoticed internationally. The German Legation at Berne reported in detail on the ongoing efforts of Swiss organizations raising relief funds. At the same time, influential German Catholic and Protestant circles organized appeals to Bethmann Hollweg. In his cautiously worded response, the chancellor publicly assured the petitioners that he would do everything possible on behalf of the persecuted. Consequently, the Foreign Office found itself in a position that made it impossible to refuse to help Schuchardt, although it could be sure that the Ottoman ally would not appreciate the visit of the missionary to Constantinople. The Foreign Office could at least hope to control Schuchardt's activities and limit possible political damage originating from his visit.[71]

Missionary Diplomacy at Constantinople

Shortly after Schuchardt had arrived in Constantinople, the Foreign Office's calculations seemed to have suffered a serious setback. On 11 November 1915 Zimmermann sent a report to the embassy at Constantinople, informing the staff that Schuchardt seemed to have broken earlier agreements. A German missionary journal had published information on the Armenian Genocide that the Foreign Office had earlier shared with the Hülfsbund. It took some time before the new ambassador, Count Paul Wolff-Metternich, informed his enraged superiors that Schuchardt was not the source of the indiscretion.[72] By that time Schuchardt had collected abundant new information on the deportations and massacres. Moreover he had several meetings in Constantinople. He had met with Peet who urged him to visit Morgenthau. On 12 November 1915 Mrs. Peet accompanied Schuchardt to the American embassy. In his diaries, Morgenthau noted that although Schuchardt was well informed on the atrocities, he still tried to justify the Ottoman government's policy to some extent. Nevertheless, Schuchardt, Peet, and Morgenthau kept in contact. Following a lunch date on 17 November, Schuchardt brought Beatrice Rohner, who had arrived from Marash, to Morgenthau to report on her experiences. It is evident that the relations between the Hülfsbund and leading United States circles in the Ottoman capital were excellent.[73]

The Ottoman government had tried its best to prevent such meetings throughout the year. When Schuchardt discussed his initial travel plans with the German Foreign Office, Karl Blank and Beatrice Rohner also applied for travel permits to meet him at Constantinople. The Ottoman provincial authorities, however, had no interest that these two eyewitnesses should travel to Constantinople. Djemal Pasha did not grant the travel permits. The official reason was that the roads were unsafe, although the two would have traveled by rail and on the military supply route to the Ottoman capital. Rössler did not accept this reasoning and asked the embassy to intervene on behalf of the Hülfsbund. The Hülfsbund itself assisted the diplomatic efforts by canceling Blank's application for a travel permit. Blank had politically exposed himself during the Zeitoun affair. Finally, on the orders of the Foreign Office, the travel permit for Rohner was secured.[74]

During their talks Schuchardt and Peet decided to intensify their cooperation and coordinated the relief work of their organizations into one effort. The obvious importance of Aleppo as a center for deportees pointed strongly to the need to establish relief work at that place. Neither a Hülfsbund nor an ABCFM station existed in the city. An ABCFM missionary, Dr. Fred Shepard, had arrived in Aleppo from Aintab. He had tried stopping the deportations through appeals to the governor of Aleppo. In response, the governor had advised him that the orders had come from Constantinople. Shepard thus went on to the capital, but he did not achieve anything. He was, however, able to take back with him some relief funds. From Aleppo he sent a detailed report on his trip and the immediate relief work he had been undertaking. The missionaries in Adana and Tarsus were unable to provide regular relief to the deportees passing through these places. The distribution depended largely on Armenian intermediaries willing to take up the work. Dr. Haas at the American Hospital in Adana had provided 400 Turkish pounds for the work. It was encouraging that the Baghdad Railway company had agreed to forward funds through its channels, thereby facilitating the work. Shepard left no doubt that Aleppo had to be the future center of the work:

> Aleppo is the great center from which to do relief work and the need is beyond estimate. The 150,000 or more refugees will, I suppose, pass on through here; they are now on the road between Konia and Aleppo. There are large numbers in the city now, and large numbers within

reach from here. Trustworthy native friends are able to use consid-
erable sums—in small amounts. . . . There is unfortunately no way to
reach effectively the many thousands en route. 10,000, between
Bozanti and Tarsus; 20,000 at Tarsus; 40,000 between Osmanieh and
Islohia; (which is now the head of the rail) and 40-50,000 at Kotmoh.
. . . Typhus has broken out here.[75]

Given that the German Hülfsbund could hope for some German government support and consequently fewer problems with the Ottoman government, it seemed that Hülfsbund personnel, rather than ABCFM workers,
should build up the relief network in the area. Thus, Peet and Schuchardt
entrusted the work to Paula Schäfer, a nurse,[76] and Beatrice Rohner, an ed-
ucator,[77] both members of the Hülfsbund's Marash station.

Organizing the Armenian Relief Effort at Aleppo

The arrival of deportees' caravans shocked the Armenian communities of
Aleppo, which set out to provide relief. The first steps in providing relief
were ad hoc measures to deal with the most urgent and immediate needs
of the new arrivals. But it soon became clear that the emergency was not a
temporary phenomenon; it would be a long-lasting crisis.

Reverend Hovhannes Eskijian, the pastor of the Emmanuel Evangelical
Church of Aleppo, proved to be the key player in organizing the local relief
effort. Although he was relatively young and had only been in the town for
two years, he was an experienced organizer. During earlier stint as pastor
to the Armenian village of Ekizoluk, he had coped with the effects of the
1909 massacres. During the Adana massacres many Armenian villages in the
area where Ekizoluk was situated had been burned down by Muslim mobs.
While the loss of life remained limited in comparison to the slaughters on
the Cilician plains, the already-poor villagers had serious problems regaining
their economic self-sufficiency.[78] In 1913 the Protestant Armenians of Aleppo invited Eskijian to join them. From the beginning, Eskijian impressed the
Aleppo community with is organizational skills. He formed a Christian youth
society, a Sunday school, and a series of social meetings.[79] Thus, the young
reverend placed the emphasis of his work on the education of his community's youth and the molding of a unified membership. Like his experience
with the relief and reconstruction work at Ekizoluk, these programs prepared him and the community for the tremendous challenge ahead.

When in the summer 1915 the disaster hit Aleppo, Eskijian understood
that his efforts must not be limited to his own Protestant community. Over-

coming all differences that had separated the different local Armenian communities in previous years, Eskijian contributed to the creation of a unified Armenian relief effort. He worked together with Father Haroutune Yayian of the Armenian Apostolic Church in the distribution of relief funds.

A unified Armenian relief effort was certainly indispensable, but additional help was badly needed. Luckily, other local Ottoman citizens joined the work. Particularly valuable were volunteers who had the opportunity to travel in the country around Aleppo and

Hagop Haleblian

deliver relief funds and collect information about the ongoing murder of the deportees. Hagop Haleblian, for example, was fluent in Arabic and Kurdish. He changed his dress and tattooed his hands and face according to local Kurdish and Arab customs. Indistinguishable from a local Kurd or Arab, Haleblian managed to obtain a position as a watchman for the Baghdad Railway company, guarding the Euphrates railway bridge at Djerablus. His work allowed him to keep contact with Artin Vanes, the Armenian interpreter of a German officer. In the winter of 1915–16, with the help of this interpreter,

Haleblian succeeded in convincing the officer that some relief work would be possible. The officer not only gave his consent and a strongly worded travel permit for Haleblian, but also instructed his interpreter to write an appeal in Armenian for clothes and other necessities to Eskijian. The reverend was very pleased by Haleblian's arrival in Aleppo. The newcomer was capable of providing essential services to the underground network thanks to his perfect disguise and official travel permits. From now on, Haleblian carried letters and money between Aleppo and relief workers in smaller places. In Aleppo, the mail was tied to Haleblian's body so as to avoid detection in case of police controls. This way, the relief work along the Euphrates could be sustained for some time, until Eskijian's death.[80]

Hovhannes Eskijian

Another important local personality who supported the relief effort was Selim Effendi, a police officer of Albanian decent who actively obstructed the searches for Armenian hiding places. The officer informed Eskijian ahead of time and also saw to it that the searches were conducted in places where no Armenian fugitives were hiding at a given moment. While no precise information is available on the extent of Muslim participation in the activities of the underground network, Selim Effendi's role demonstrates that the humanitarian resistance at Aleppo was not limited to the non-Muslim communities. The participation of Muslims like Selim Effendi also shows that the Ottoman provincial administration could not count on the allegiance of all its officials. Therefore, any general administrative measure became quickly known to the underground.[81]

Rev. Eflatoon Elmajian

The majority of Armenians in hiding were deported families or women with children. They came to Eskijian because they had heard of his humanitarian work prior to reaching Aleppo. After her awful experiences at Katma, Naomie Ouzounian fell sick and hardly managed to regain her strength. When she got back on her feet, she tried to escape from a transit camp on her way to Der Zor. The camp was rather close to Aleppo, so it was probably in the Kasildik area.[82] Although she did not know the way to the city, she followed a number of guards and military personnel, as she believed that these men were walking back to the city. However, the guards discovered her escape and pursued her. Naomie ran for her life but the guards were faster. Only the intervention of a Muslim preacher prevented her from being dragged back to the camp. On the inquiries of the imam about her wishes, she answered that "they are talking about a Christian pastor who has devoted his life to saving as many orphans and helpless sick old people as he can. I want to find him and help to save my family from being taken to Deir-el-Zor. His name is Rev. Eskijian. 'Oh, yes,' he said, 'I have heard of the saintly man myself. I happen to know where he lives.' He helped me into his carriage, gave the driver some instructions and he started to walk. He is a Moslem. How come he tries to help me? He must have kindness and charity in his heart towards a frightened helpless child. He must be a godly man.'" The driver brought the girl to Eskijian's house, where she had to wait outside for the return of the reverend. "Finally just before darkness set in, the gate opened and he walked in, a young man. He couldn't have been over thirty-five, a handsome man, with attractive dark eyes and fair complexion. But he was a tired man, a very, very tired looking man. He turned to me and as if he knew I would be there, he said, 'I am sorry to be late. Have you been waiting long? We had a very large load of children brought in from the camp today. They were all very sick with typhus and dysentery. They had to be cleaned, fed, and put to bed in the orphanage. There was a shortage of clean clothes, bedding and medication. Anyway, come in with me and lets both clean up a bit and have dinner, then we can talk.'" Three days after her arrival, Hovannes Effendi, a native of Aleppo, fluent in Arabic, and coworker of Eskijian, endeavored to get Naomie's family out of the camp. He dressed as a mortician and smuggled Naomie's relatives to Aleppo, where the family went into hiding with Eskijian's help. After some time the family had to be distributed to several different hiding places. Naomie went to live with an Arab Catholic family and took care of the children. Later she managed, like many Armenian women in Aleppo, to be accepted as a nurse in an Ottoman military hospital.[83]

While helping all of these victims, Eskijian organized shelters for specific groups on a systematic basis. Teenage boys were a prime target for the local police, so the reverend saw to it that as many of these boys as possible were placed in secure locations, where they could also assist in the relief work. One of the boys working in this way was Sarkis Consulian, who was sixteen when he had been accepted in Eskijian's orphanage.[84]

Rev. Sarkis Consulian

The other most-wanted group of Armenians targeted by the authorities consisted of those who had a college education. One such person was Eflatoon E. Elmajian who had, like Eskijian, graduated from the Marash Theological Seminary. When Eskijian learned that Elmajian had managed to reach Aleppo and gone into hiding, the former sought him out and arranged safer quarters for him, drawing considerable danger upon himself in the process. For six months the underground network provided Elmajian with daily food and often smuggled him to new hiding places when older ones became unsafe. At one point an Arab Christian family had accepted a large sum of money from Eskijian for housing Elmajian. After one week the host went to the local authorities and denounced Elmajian, telling the police that a prison escapee was hiding in his house.[85]

One day Eskijian explained his relief program to Minassian:

> You must know that there are too little funds to go around. This is a gigantic task, saving so many people from destruction. The war is going to last a long time yet, and we are trying to choose whom to save, since we can't possibly save all. Our plan is for the future, and the future is for the young men of your age. Regardless of what effort we may exert, young children will die. But by protecting groups of your age, we are confident that you will survive and that you will build a new generation, the future of Armenia."[86]

Elmajian escaped from the house in time, however, and Eskijian placed him in another Arab house. The new landlord betrayed Elmajian as well. Finally, Eskijian brought the fugitive to a house where a secret shelter had been created, hidden behind a kitchen wall. The place was safe enough for Elmajian to stay a whole month. The precautions were very important, as the police had Armenian officers on staff and also employed Armenian informants.

A certain Arshavir was particularly notorious and feared by the deportees. According to Elmajian, Arshavir received a set sum for every fugitive Armenian he could catch. One afternoon, at the end of December 1915, Elmajian was reading outside the secret shelter, in the living room of his landlady's apartment. Suddenly he realized that three police officers had come into the house. The young man kept an outwardly cool attitude and simply walked past the men upstairs to the flat roof, whence he jumped into a neighboring yard and made his way to Eskijian's house once more. After this narrow escape, he left Aleppo to seek refuge like many other young Armenian men on the German-run construction sites of the Baghdad Railway line.[87]

Before Elmajian made his escape from Aleppo he had helped Eskijian for several months, often living in the Eskijian house. There, Elmajian saw the unending stream of deportees knocking on the reverend's door looking for a piece of bread or some other help. At the same time, Eskijian used the temporary exemption of Protestants from deportation to claim as many young Armenians as possible as Protestants, irrespective of their real religious affiliation.[88] Since most of the deportees arrived in unscheduled trains at Aleppo, it was imperative to monitor the arrival of trains as well as possible. Sometimes, Eskijian had to leave his work abruptly or get up in the middle of the night to go to the train station and rescue newly arriving deportees. Elmajian recalls:

> One day, around lunch time, hearing the whistle, he ran out of the house, and jumping into a horse drawn carriage he rushed to meet the train. As he walked through the freight cars which were jammed with refugees, he noticed a group of women huddled together in a strange manner. When he approached them, he saw a few scantily clad young ladies sitting on the floor of the wagon and these women were huddling around them to keep their nakedness from the eyes of the onlookers. Rev. Eskijian was unprepared to cope with this strange situation. However, he and the helper with him took off their jackets to cover two of these young ladies, and managing to cover the rest of them with any old thing he could put his hand on, brought them to his home. Immediately, gowns were made for them for temporary use until proper clothing could be supplied. Thus, the care of daily increasing numbers of refugees was growing to be a problem for Rev. Eskijian, tiring him tremendously.[89]

On days when Eskijian could not go to the railway station himself, he sent Hovhannes Juskalian. "He spoke perfect Turkish, some Armenian, and good Arabic. He would bring back people who wanted to be called Protestants, even if they were not actually Protestants. The reverend knew of the ruse, but asked no questions. He wanted to save lives before he saved souls."

At times, "the Reverend was incredulous at the number of members of his denomination, but Hovhaness Effendi would calmly and with his usual aplomb, tell the Reverend that he too was surprised. Sometimes he would say jokingly, 'They are new members,' and would whisper in the Reverend's ear: 'I baptized them myself.'"[90]

Garabed Keverian had worked as a volunteer for Eskijian. As his secretary, he knew the reverend's plans intimately. He recalls: "Eskijian went to the train station. One side of the train Catholic priests and Eskijian on the other. His Grace claimed the young ones as Catholics. The Ottoman official gets angry. 'They come from the interior provinces. How do you know that they are Catholics?' 'Well, every religion has its secret sign we know that they are Catholics.' Eskijian did the same. There existed a lot of envy against the Protestants."[91]

Armenian refugees

Communication between Eskijian, the various secret shelters, physicians, and the United States consulates were important but a serious problem. John Minassian, a young deportee, looked younger than he actually was. Thus, he ran a lower risk of being arrested by the police. Eskijian made him his messenger between the railway station and his house. Dressed like a local Arab, Minassian also escorted the sick to physicians and transported material between the various locations. It was particularly dangerous to supply the United States consulate with information on the massacres. At times, Eskijian visited Jackson personally and urged him to secure more relief funds through United States embassy channels. One day during a meeting at the consulate, Jackson shared with Eskijian information that he had received through his diplomatic channels. He urged the reverend to prepare for even more deportees, as he had learned that Armenian deportees from Sivas, Kharpert, and Malatia were on their way to Aleppo, and that their condition was much worse than what the two men had seen so far.[92] Usually, however, the two men avoided direct contact and communicated through Minassian. "I got to know most of the important people in town who enjoyed the protection of the reverend's one-man army. I began delivering messages in folded envelopes to Mr. Jackson, the American Consul, who, when evening fell, would send his first secretary to visit Reverend Eskijian to leave him a small canvas bag. The reverend, in turn, would give the secretary a heavy typewritten envelope prepared by his secretaries, hidden in the basement and who seldom came up for fresh air."[93]

Among the important locations for deportees, aside from the train station, were a number of khans in the city. Before the war, these had been used by local enterprises for artisanal production and the putting-out system of industry. With the collapse of production, the premises became available to the local authorities to concentrate Armenian deportees in them. Many of the sick, undernourished, and exhausted people died in these inns and were carried off daily to the mass graves. Walter Geddes, an eyewitness from the United States, had visited these places:

> If one looks into these places where they are living one simply sees a huddled mass of dying and dead, all mixed up with discarded, ragged clothing, refuse and human excrement, and it is impossible to pick out any one portion and describe it as being a living person. A number of open carts used to parade the streets, looking out for corpses, and it was a common sight to see one of these carts pass containing anything up to ten or twelve human bodies, all terribly emaciated. These carts have since been provided with a lid and painted black, and one constantly sees bodies, mostly of women and children, being dragged out of courtyards and alleyways and thrown into them as one would throw a sack of coal. It is impossible to gauge the number of deaths per diem, but in the Armenian Cemetery trenches are dug and the bodies are simply brought there and thrown in indiscriminately. A number of priests remain at the cemetery all day, and perform some kind of funeral rite as the so-called interment is made.[94]

John Minassian had witnessed these scenes too: "Once they had been like nature's gift to humanity, but now the sanitation department simply picked them up and carted them off to the garbage dump, covering them with lye to make certain they were dead. The reverend tried to absorb as much of the misery as he could, to counteract the unspeakable crime organized by the Turkish government."[95]

Returning one day from these houses of death, Eskijian was particularly depressed and refused to speak. He sat silently in the kitchen and refused to eat.

> After staying motionless for about 15 minutes, he suddenly burst into tears crying and sobbing aloud. We left him alone to weep. After quieting down, he left us. We did not know where he was going, neither thought it wise to follow him. It was not very long before he returned with two little children under each arm. Calling Mrs. Eskijian, he asked her to clean and feed them. Again he went away, and with three such trips he brought six children. Soon we understood the cause of his abnormal state of mind. That day, late in the afternoon, he had visited one of these houses of industry where the workers had not stopped for a few days to pick up the dead. He saw quite a number of dead mothers and small children lying besides some of them. Looking closely, he discovered that the mothers were all dead but some of the children still had life in them. Evidently these mothers fed their children with all they had and died of starvation, but their children, though near death, were still alive. When Rev. Eskijian saw these small children clinging to their dead mothers, his nerves were shattered, his mind was frozen, and his whole physical system was grief stricken. It was these little children that he had brought home for Mrs. Eskijian to clean and feed. The children were filthy and badly infested with hundreds of lice. They were taken to the church yard where Mrs. Eskijian, with several other helpers, tried to clean them and feed them with light baby meals. This was that start of an orphanage in Aleppo which was another heavy burden for Rev. Eskijian to carry in addition to many other responsibilities he was shouldering.[96]

The orphanage work attempted to save as many as possible of the Armenian orphans who were wandering around in the streets of Aleppo. Many of the children had been left behind by their families when these were deported from Aleppo to Der Zor. The mothers had hoped to save their children this way.[97] In the orphanage, a group of workers devoted itself "to healing, clothing, washing, and substituting as mothers and teachers, each in her or his own language, either Armenian or Turkish. Each day a few died, and each day more orphans came, as if this were the lighthouse in a seaport of desperation. At least they were not outside, subjected to harassment. This was especially true for the teenage girls and young widows."[98]

Elmajian believed that Reverend Eskijian contracted typhus while carrying the lice-infected orphans to his orphanage, and finally died of the disease.[99] He died on 25 March 1916, after a short illness. Within days, letters were smuggled to Aleppo from the surrounding districts and the concentration camps of the desert. The information system was functioning well at that time and the deportees had learned soon about the death of their supporter. The compassionate letters praised the deceased as a national leader.[100]

After the reverend's death the critical importance of his main supporter, his wife Gulenia, became evident. She drew strength to face the challenges her young family was encountering from her strong religious beliefs. Besides doing laundry and cooking for many deportees in hiding, and running her own household, she also did a lot of clerical work for the relief effort. When her husband was absent, she managed the work at the house. In view of the constant threat of police searches, this was a dangerous task. At times, she needed all her skills to obstruct such searches.[101]

Armenian refugees

Mrs. Eskijian was instrumental in hiding many Armenian girls and attending to their needs. It was she who established contacts with Muslim women and placed the girls in those households. Once a girl had found shelter this way,

Mrs. Eskijian maintained contact with the girl. This networking among the women of Aleppo was efficient, as the danger of detection by the police was somewhat limited. The Ottoman police had no female officers and betrayals seemed not to have happened. The direct negotiating with Muslim wives secured, the consent of the women was indispensable for the success of this work.[102]

After her husband's death, Mrs. Eskijian took over the leadership of the relief effort. She assumed this central role in the underground work undisputed. This indicates that her previous work was fully appreciated by the other important local figures such as Consul Jackson. As a first measure to keep the orphanage work running, she named an elderly man as director. But the police arrested him soon and he disappeared. Looking for a replacement, Mrs. Eskijian decided that an underground supporter from Aintab College should fill the vacancy. But he also survived only a short while; the police took him away as well. Finally, only the reverend's trusted messenger, Minassian, was left to take on the task, although he did not have the necessary experience.[103] Clearly, the number of surviving volunteers had shrunk to only a handful. Minassian managed to hold out in his new positions for some time. But the authorities had decided to put an end to the Armenian relief work.

> Our orphanage was raided time and again, all the older and teenage girls were taken until we were not able to continue. I was advised to leave my job for safety. Mrs. Rohner assigned me to work as a teacher in her orphanage, and thus enjoy her protection and security. My friend Haroutun asked me to join other boys, and live with them, who were also teaching classes at the orphanage. Then we heard that the police had picked up about thirty-five young boys from the orphanage, all under fifteen years of age, and sent them to Turkish schools to be raised as Turks. Kagham was one of them. When they tried to circumcise the boys, a few ran away for this was the worst insult for an Armenian boy. Some children came to Mrs. Rohner's orphanage for safety, since her position as a German missionary offered privilege and protection.[104]

With the last attempt to save at least some of the orphans, Eskijian's relief effort ended. Minassian survived for some time under Rohner's protection but soon he too had to escape from Aleppo. Rohner advised him that she could no longer protect him. Minassian left to work on the Baghdad Railway construction and was one of the few who had joined the Eskijian relief effort who survived the Genocide.[105]

Eskijian had presumably died just in time to avoid arrest. The police had already interrogated him about his work. He had turned to Rohner for help, and she had managed to stop the inquiry for some time, but it was clear that the danger was never over.[106] The ruthless persecution of his successors show that his work was no longer tolerated. The raids on his orphanage and arrests of the personnel and abduction of the girls formed part of a comprehensive roundup of Armenians in Aleppo in the spring of 1916. Eskijian had anticipated the coming extermination campaign. He had been preparing plans for an "underground railway," transferring Armenian deportees from the Syrian desert to the safe heaven of the areas controlled by Dersim Kurds.[107]

Eskijian's work was a critical step in the development of the relief effort at Aleppo. He identified the survival of Armenian intellectuals, orphans, and other young Armenians as the major object of relief work. Therefore, his work was not solely a humanitarian initiative but also a program for Armenian national survival. Eskijian's underground network survived for about nine months, until it was destroyed by the local Ottoman police. This success was in part due to his ability to link his initiative with an international relief effort. This broader relief program not only sustained Eskijian's work financially but also followed closely his programmatic approach.

The International Relief Effort and Orphanage Work at Aleppo

On her way back from the meetings in Constantinople, Rohner visited a transit camp for Armenian deportees near the railway station at Mamoure. Paula Schäfer, a missionary colleague, was already working along the route. The conditions of the deportees had not improved, and the winter cold increased the death toll among them considerably.[108] By December 1915 the two women attempted to extend their work to Aleppo. Rohner wrote to the German embassy, requesting the dispatch of two Red Cross nurses. She added that the "Americans" were willing to finance relief work if something could be done in secret. Since she asked that the reply to the request be sent to the German consulate at Aleppo, it was evident that preparations were well under way. At Aleppo, Schäfer and Rohner sought Djemal Pasha's permission for their work among the deportees, emphasizing the importance of the relief effort for the overall sanitary conditions in the city. The general declined, however. Nevertheless, Rohner did not give up. When she approached Djemal a second time about a week later, the official still declined her request but made an offer.[109]

Von Kress had also been working to improve the situation for the Armenian deportees. In December 1915 he managed to show Djemal the conditions under which Armenians orphans were kept by the local authorities in Aleppo. In a primitive shelter with a broken roof, five hundred Armenian children died slowly of hunger and exposure. Ottoman officials had stolen the donations that the local population had made. Djemal was visibly shocked by what he saw, as tears ran down his face. He agreed to use army supplies to provide food and clothing to the children. The German community leader Koch and his wife, who had been trying to support and save Armenians since the beginning of the deportations, extended an invitation for breakfast to Djemal for 21 December 1915. Besides Koch, Djemal, and Kress, Föllner, the director of the Baghdad Railway construction at Aleppo, and Busse, a high-ranking German navy commander newly delegated to Djemal's staff, were present. At the meeting Djemal gave the exceptional permission that the orphan work might come under German direction by 23 December. Learning of the general's decision, the local police tried to deport all children in the evening of 22 December. The German colony suspected that the police tried sabotaging the relief effort because the officials profited from the sale of Armenian girls from the orphanage.[110]

In response to the affront, Djemal offered Rohner permission to take over the organization of an orphanage in a former French convent. Rohner estimated that about 50 percent of the children had already died in the place. With an urgent telegram, she secured Schuchardt's permission to accept 250 children on the condition that the Ottoman army would provide the necessary supplies.[111] The number of orphans rose quickly to 320, but almost every day some children died. In the first phase of the organization, Schäfer assisted Rohner. While focusing on the orphan work, both women did not forget their original plan. The orphanage provided them with the necessary permit to stay in Aleppo. Having secured their position at Aleppo, they arranged with the United States and German consulates for the delivery of relief supplies to deportees in the outlying concentration camps and elsewhere. Their quick expansion of the relief work was unthinkable without the earlier efforts of Eskijian and others. In short, the infrastructure for the distribution of funds was already in place when the funds from abroad arrived at Aleppo. Soon, Rohner and Schäfer needed additional funds for their work. They appealed to Peet in Constantinople, who administered the incoming donations from the United States. An important project was collecting Armenian orphans in their whole Aleppo region. To achieve this objective, Peet had to guarantee their upkeep until the conclusion of peace.[112]

The transfer of money and information between Aleppo and Constantinople was generally organized through the United States consulate. Consul Jackson administered considerable sums that were usually forwarded by Peet to the Aleppo branch of the German Orient Bank and kept there on hold for Jackson. Naturally, the Ottoman authorities had a strong interest in learning more about the relief effort, since the ABCFM and the Hülfsbund had not received official permission for such work. Thus, Jackson urged Peet to avoid sending letters by standard mail and instead to use the United States diplomatic mail service. Jackson did not know that United States diplomatic mail had been compromised. Ottoman authorities had already opened the sealed mail of the United States consulate at Kharpert at least since August 1915.[113]

On receipt, the consul passed the funds on to Schäfer and Rohner, while Schäfer also withdrew funds directly at Adana when she traveled in that region. Both women submitted regular accounts of expenditures to Peet. They also passed on substantial sums to Eskijian for direct distribution. In other words, a considerable part of the international relief work was administered independently by local Armenians.[114]

The need for funds was huge. On 2 January 1916 Rohner used the good offices of Rössler to cable an urgent appeal to Peet by way of the German embassy at Constantinople. Rohner estimated a weekly payment of 500 Turkish pounds to be the minimum for meeting the most urgent needs. On 6 January 1916 Metternich informed Rössler that Peet could guarantee 1,000 pounds until the end of February. Thus, the available funds were seriously limited given the tasks relief workers were facing. In view of the difficulties Rohner and her coworkers faced, Metternich regarded the situation as an opportune moment for contributing to the relief effort. Two hundred pounds had been allocated to Rössler for that purpose already earlier in October and November. Now, Metternich sent 500 pounds to the consulate at Aleppo. He insisted that the funds had to be distributed separately by Rössler as a distinct German effort. The measure formed part of the government's attempts to enhance its damaged image. Morgenthau had also made it clear that he wanted to see some German contribution. The limited German assistance could not, however, meet the constantly increasing demand for funds. Rössler used the incoming government contributions to finance, for some time, an illegal orphanage that the German community had established in a house owned by Germans. Rössler gave his tacit but still visible support for the effort so that the local police did not hinder the work. Rössler gave another part of the 500 pounds to Rohner for her orphanage, arguing that this way her work would obtain a more distinctly German aspect. While Metternich did not comment explicitly on the very limited extent of German aid for the Armenians, he did not fail to point out this fact to his superiors once the opportunity presented itself.[115]

On 17 January 1916 Metternich informed Rohner that Peet urged her to send relief to the Armenian deportees at Bab, where a concentration camp existed.[116] In sum, by January the original plans for the relief work had to be modified according to the conditions in and around Aleppo. Consequently, Jackson proposed a change, describing the desperate situation at length:

> The Protestant community here is establishing orphanages in Maara, Hama, Homs, Selimia, Ras-el-Ain, Djissr-el-Chougr, and Deir-el-Zor, at which places they are picking up the best of the straggling children that are left without any parents. Five or six are already running in Aleppo. They say that there are at least 300,000 helpless and starving people of all kinds in the vicinity of Deir-el-Zor alone (to say nothing of the thousands in other localities), and if there are, which I do not doubt, as there has been every effort made to send practically all of the Armenians to that place for more than a month, the needs are beyond calculation. Relief is being distributed without any regard to the church to which people belong, Gregorian, Protestant and Catholic all being treated alike. It is safe to say, however, that the Protestants have by far the best organization and the most able workers, but the Gregorians outnumber them by far.
>
> To make a long story short, it requires many thousands of pounds a week to only partially meet the needs, and as I have no means of knowing what your resources are, I must leave it to you to supply what you can. It goes without saying that you will do your best to save at least a remnant of this unfortunate people. They are dying by the thousands every day for they have neither shelter, food, clothing, or medical attendance, and the desire of the guilty to entirely exterminate them bids fair to succeed unless drastic measures are taken.
>
> Misses Schaeffer and Rohner are not in a position to do general relief work, as I thought they would do, and are using the funds they get for the orphanages under their care principally, so money should be sent to me to give to the heads of the communities "en block," and not much in detail except in rare cases. Miss Rohner has had her hands tied by taking over a Government orphanage. Aintab has as yet not decided if they can send some one, so I must continue as above stated. Send me regularly and as much as possible, and I will divide the money among the communities and orphanages as I think best, if this meets your approval. I have five times as much as I should do, but will take care of this end if you will furnish the funds. Please talk this over with Mr. Morgenthau, and if possible wire me a stated sum weekly."[117]

The Ottoman Government's Counter Measures and the Struggle for the Orphans

While the relief work expanded rapidly in the districts surrounding Aleppo and along the Euphrates, Rohner's orphan work was by no means firmly established. Shortly after the start of the work, rumors abounded that the authorities would take away the boys from the orphanage.[118] The rumors were well founded. Rössler ascertained that the government had been planning to send all Armenian orphans from Aleppo to government orphanages at Constantinople. Only adverse winter weather had forced the authorities to postpone their plans. Rössler explained to Metternich that the measure would destroy the German relief effort. He left it to the ambassador to conclude that the desired effect for German image would suffer as well.[119]

The planned removal of the orphans coincided with elimination of the concentration camp at Bab and the preparations for renewed deportations from Aleppo and the districts in the city's vicinity as well. The local authorities and the officials of the IAMM forced the deportees to move on further south along the Euphrates on to Der Zor. The results were devastating. Detailed reports on the death toll soon reached the German consulate. Rössler was particularly upset, as the underground organization that had been run by Eskijian and supported by him and Rohner had succeeded in sending Armenian couriers to the concentration camp and distributing funds. The relief had been insufficient, however, and could not secure the survival of many. Within two and half days of the courier's visit, 1,029 deportees died of "natural" causes.[120]

Rohner used the breathing space the winter weather had provided her to attempt to bring the orphans more securely under German protection. Armenian children in other orphanages of the Hülfsbund had been exempted from deportations and remained under German care. Therefore, Rohner sought to establish a similar arrangement for her orphans at Aleppo. A major concern was the critical financial situation. Once her organization could provide all funds for her orphanage, Rohner could claim German protection for the children. At the same time, the upkeep of the children would no longer come out of the limited relief budget. On 22 February Rohner cabled to Schuchardt in Frankfurt and inquired whether the Hülfsbund would be willing to fully finance one to two hundred Armenian orphans. The next day, Rössler sent an urgent telegram to the embassy informing Metternich that the governor of Aleppo had informed Rohner that the government would take over control of all orphans. Rössler estimated the number of orphans at about one thousand, of which about four hundred were under Rohner's care. The latter had learned that contrary to the government's announcement, the authorities did not intend to send the children to Constantinople but to Sivas. She concluded that this would amount to child murder.[121]

The Ottoman authorities' move came at a most unfortunate moment for the German Foreign Office. The Swiss circles that had organized a relief organization had officially requested German support. They planned to become directly active in the Ottoman interior provinces. In response Undersecretary of State Zimmermann assured the petitioners that their ultimate intentions were identical to those of his government. For a variety of reasons, however, he saw no possibility for the Swiss to travel to Aleppo. Nevertheless, Zimmermann argued that the petitioners could achieve their objectives by making their funds and other resources available to the Foreign Office for further distribution. Therefore, a deportation of Rohner's Armenian orphans would not only make any relief effort appear meaningless but would also result in a significant loss of face for the German government internationally. Consequently, Zimmermann authorized Metternich to intervene on behalf of the children. The ambassador immediately instructed Rössler to further inquire into the Ottoman authorities plans concerning the orphans. Within a few days, Rössler could report that the Ottoman authorities had postponed their plans for the time being. He stressed, however, that Rohner's presence in Aleppo was instrumental for the security of the children and refused to take any responsibility if she would leave the city even temporarily.[122]

While the struggle for the orphans was in full swing, the lack of available funds further aggravated the situation at Aleppo. Jackson had not received news or funds from Peet for some time. As he had no way to send coded telegrams, he approached Rössler and used the latter's good offices for an urgent appeal to the ABCFM. Peet reacted promptly, but transferred the money to Schäfer, who was absent. Thus, Rössler again had to help out and requested that the ABCFM change the order to Jackson's name. The money had hardly arrived when Rohner urgently appealed for an extra allocation of 200 Turkish pounds. She had secured a way to send the money to Der Zor, where forty thousand Armenians were concentrated. At that time, Peet transferred 500 pounds to Jackson each week.[123]

The distribution of relief funds could not be hidden completely from the eyes of the authorities. Ottoman military intelligence had ascertained that aid committees in the United States had forwarded relief funds to the United

States embassy at Constantinople for further distribution. Therefore, on 21 January 1916, the Ottoman general staff requested the Ministry of the Interior to conduct a "serious investigation" into the matter and find out more about the secret distribution of funds. On 30 January Talaat sent a circular telegram to all provinces and independent districts where there had been deportation of Armenians. He ordered a "secret and serious" investigation into the distribution of funds. Of special importance was to learn who the actual distributors were.[124]

The Ministry of the Interior's Directorate for Public Security followed the relief effort as closely as possible. In those areas where missionaries or United States consuls were active, local authorities had to file detailed reports on the relief activities.[125] Talaat was particularly concerned that United States citizens or non-Muslim Ottoman citizens who did not enjoy the trust of the Ottoman government were traveling as merchants in the Lower Euphrates region. In other words, news had reached Constantinople that foreigners, and most likely Armenian volunteers, were making their way into those districts that the Ottoman government had earlier designated as Armenian "settlement areas." Talaat ordered the authorities in the region to impede such journeys.[126] Soon he had learned that the distribution of relief funds was not limited to United States institutions and that German missionary circles were participating in the effort as well. The minister stressed that only Ottoman officials were entitled to distribute money to deportees. Distributions by others had to be stopped.[127] Given that Talaat had expressed his orders in no uncertain terms, it must have been disturbing to him to learn that some local officials had turned a blind eye to the relief effort. Some officials even seemed to have actually given permission for relief work. In a circular telegram dated 3 April 1916, Talaat emphasized that on the orders of Enver Pasha, those officials had to be punished severely. Evidently, helping Armenians or being lenient in humanitarian matters was a major offence in the eyes of the Ottoman government.[128]

When Djemal Pasha was ordered to put an end to the relief work, he confidentially informed the German consul at Damascus about his instructions. He argued that the distributions were contrary to the political interests of the state. The foreign aid had to stop in order to demonstrate to the Armenians that they could not hope for any assistance from abroad and hence had to give up their political aspirations. Nevertheless, Djemal assured the consul that he personally wanted to help the deportees and would be willing to arrange for the distribution of relief money through his officials. To show his goodwill, Djemal immediately ordered, in the presence of the German consul, the organization of an orphanage for Armenian children. Metternich, however, learned that the Ottoman government tried also to prevent the Apostolic Armenian patriarchate at Constantinople from helping the deportees. Therefore, the patriarch was forced to take recourse to the help of foreigners, who would bring the assistance to the deportees. It seemed that the government's reasons were other than those stated.[129]

The Deportations of Spring 1916

By the end of March, the authorities began to deport toward Der Zor those Armenians who had still been left behind in areas on the fringes of the desert—such as in Aleppo. In preparation for these new deportations, the local authorities began to register all Armenians who were in the city. Police officers declared that the only way to escape deportation would be conversion to Islam. On 6 April Rössler reported shocking news of a large massacre of Armenian deportees at Ras-ul-Ain that had been perpetrated by Chechens on the order of the government. Metternich suspected that the Ottoman government was trying to dispose of the Armenians before the end of the war.[130]

The accelerated deportations put the relief workers into an increasingly critical position. All calculations were obsolete. Rohner implored Peet to send more money to Jackson at short intervals. Peet sent what he could, but in late April the funds were largely exhausted and further help depended on incoming donations. Rohner's description of the situation was bleak. She expected that the cost for feeding the orphans would soon rise to 50 Turkish pounds a day. The Ottoman authorities had stopped supplying food for the children at Rohner's orphanage, contrary to Djemal's guarantees. At Aleppo, she was unable to feed several hundred of deportees. About four thousand Armenians were hiding and depended fully on the foreign aid and that of their communities. People went out to the countryside to eat grass or started fighting over cadavers of dead animals lying in the streets. The good news was that a volunteer had managed to bring 400 pounds to Der Zor. The death of Reverend Eskijian and many of his helpers had weakened the local relief network considerably. Now, after the end of this Armenian Protestant orphanage, the Armenian Apostolic community was about to close their orphanage as well for want of funds. Rohner feared that the number of famine victims would soon double in the city.

Armenian refugees

Rössler was convinced that the Armenian students of the German schools at Aleppo were soon to be deported, and requested the embassy's intervention to preempt this danger. The consul pointed out that contrary to the Ottoman government's assurances that no large-scale deportations were intended, deportations were extended and an official of the IAMM played a leading role in their execution. Rössler reported that a virtual manhunt had begun in the streets. The police abducted especially girls and young women.[131]

The news arriving from the concentration camps along the Euphrates were devastating. Rohner collected the incoming information and passed it on to Peet and the German consular service. A comprehensive report by a messenger returning from the Euphrates summed up the situation:

> On the 20th of April I arrived at Meskené and found there 3500 deported Armenians, and more than 100 orphans. A part of the people have settled here as bakers and butchers etc. even tho' Meskené, is but a halting place. All the rest are begging. In every tent there are sick and dying. Any one who can not find or manage to get a piece of bread by begging, eats the grass raw and without salt. Many hundreds of the sick are left without any tent and covering in the open under the glowing sun. I saw desperate ones who threw themselves in the grave trenches and begged the grave diggers to bury them. The Government does not give the hungry any bread, and no tent to those who remain outside. As I was in Meskené, there came a caravan

of sick women and children from Bab. They are in an indescribable condition. They were thrown down from the wagons as logs. They cried for water, they were given each a piece of dry bread, and were left there. No one thought to fetch some water for them after they had remained for a day under that glowing sun. We had to work the whole night long so as to ameliorate a little their condition. Among the orphans from Bab there was a small boy of four years of age. It was early in the morning. I asked him whether he had eaten anything. He looked much amazed, and said, "I have gazed at the stars, and my dear God has satisfied me." On my question where his father and his mother were, he said simply that they were dead in the desert. In Meskené, I gathered one hundred children under a tent. I had their hair cut and had them bathed and their rags washed. They receive daily some bread and some soup. As I had to go further in six days, I saw a young widow from Hadjin, who asked me to take the children under her care. She belonged to a good family and had received a high education. She gave herself with an intense love to the children work. I found the same lady a few weeks later in Sepka clothed in rags, she had lost her wits and wandered here about and asked everyone "Where are my children, what have you done to them?" She sought bones and grass and showed them to the passers by. If you give any one some ones [?] he buys bread and tastes some of it and gives the rest to one who is hungrier than himself. Ten days after my departure, they had sent the women with the one hundred children south. In Abu Hara she spent the rest of the money and all that she herself possessed. The children were scattered, prey to hunger. In Deir-Zor I found two of the children. They, the only survivors, said that all the rest had perished. In Meskene I saw more than 600 deported who had lived in Muara till now and had spent a pitiful sojourn, of nine months. These were now once more persecuted and sent to different places. Slowly and exhausted they came on with their possessions on their backs. As food, they cook the grass, press the water out and make balls which they dry in the sun. On the first of May I came to Debsy, there I found the above mentioned six hundred deportees all in despair. They had not been allowed to rest once or to gather grass, but they had been cruelly driven on. On the way I found people dying everywhere. They had been exhausted from hunger and thirst. Those who had remained behind the caravan must perish so painfully. Every few minutes came the stench of death. The gendarmes beat these stragglers saying they pretend to be tired. In Debsy there are 3,000 deported. In Abu Hara 6,000. In both places the death rate is one percent daily. In Hama I found seven thousand deported, three thousand of them hungry and practically naked. Here there is no grass, the locusts have consumed everything. I saw how the people were gathering the locusts, and eating them raw or cooked. Others are looking for the roots of the grasses. They catch street dogs like savages, pounce upon dead animals, whose flesh they eat eagerly without cooking. They showed me how they bury the dead shallow near the tents. In Raka and suburbs, there are 15,000 deported in tents. The camp is situated on both banks of the Euphrates. But these people are not allowed to enter the city. Rich people are paying from 30-40 Ltq to get permission from those in authority to live for a length of time in the city. Everywhere the same lamentable pictures. In Sepka there are 1,500 persons who have bought the privilege of establishing themselves there. The remaining 6,000 are in a camp on the banks of the Euphrates. Here is great misery. Some throw themselves in the river in despair. In each deportation from one place to the next, at least five-six perish through the brutal ill treatment of the accompanying gendarmery. They expect to extract money from the poor and take vengeance with heavy blows when they do not receive it. Many are transported on boats on the Euphrates. In Tibne, I found 5,000 exiles, everywhere we meet caravans of deportees. In every Arabian village there are some families. And in every Arab house women and girls. At last I came to Der Zor, and I found there 15,000 deported. Here the government is giving 150 gr. of bread to every poor person daily. Children and grownups search the garbage heaps for food and whatever is chewable is eaten. At the butcher's people wait eagerly for scraps. Of every fifty persons who come from Rakka or Sepka loaded on a boat, on an average 20 arrive, often even less. At the time of my arrival the government had gathered in Der Zor 200 orphans in a house. At my departure (six weeks later) they were eight hundred. They get a little bread and some soup daily. In the meantime came 12,000 deported to Der Zor. Every day we see caravans going in the direction of Moussul. Nevertheless, at my departure there were over 30,000 Armenians at Der Zor and in the surrounding areas. Those who have means are getting permission to delay. The rest must proceed further. Investigation showed that for this delay 4-50 Ltq. must be paid. The deportees are especially badly treated in the region of Der Zor. The people are driven back and forward with whip blows and cannot even take their most urgent needs. On my return I met new caravans everywhere and the people have the appearance of lost men. Often we suddenly see a whole row of ghastly forms rising out of a grave and asking for some bread and water. They have all dug their graves and lie there waiting for death. People of better standing who cannot make up their minds to beg for a piece of bread lie in their beds when exhausted till death comes to release them. No one looks after them. In Sepka a preacher from Aintab told me that parents have often killed their children. At the Government investigation the people fought over the fact that some had eaten their children. It has happened that the dying people have been fought over in order to devour their flesh.[132]

The "Second Phase" of the Armenian Genocide

The roundup of Armenians in Aleppo and the renewed deportations of Armenians who were still living in their original places of residence in northern Syria, such as in Marash, represented the beginning of the final phase of the Armenian Genocide.[133] In the spring of 1916, the Ottoman government reviewed the results of the deportations and massacres of 1915. Talaat and his staff identified the last concentrations of Armenians outside the areas that had been marked as their final destination, the Syrian desert.[134] From May to July the central authorities coordinated the last major and particularly ferocious campaign against their Armenian victims. While instant massacres accompanied some of the final deportations, the summer months of 1916 perhaps saw the worst massacres of the Armenian Genocide along the Khabur river in the district of Der Zor. Throughout the development of the government's genocidal schemes, relief workers at Aleppo tried their best to mitigate the consequences for the victims. In a series of suicidal missions, volunteers again entered the world of the death camps to assist those who were still alive. On 10 July 1916 Ambassador Metternich informed his superiors at Berlin: "The Armenian persecutions in the eastern provinces have entered their last phase." The Ottoman government's object was "the elimination of the Armenian Question through the extermination of the Armenian race."[135]

The deportations into the desert and the misery in the concentration camps made the utmost demands on relief workers. By the end of May, Rohner estimated the weekly needs at 2,500 Turkish pounds. But the demand rose quickly and Rohner had to ask for more. Rössler considered those who had to leave Aleppo as doomed to death.[136] Meanwhile, the governor of Aleppo informed the local Germans that the 1,400 Armenian orphans in Aleppo would be taken over by the ruling Committee of Union and Progress and sent to Konya, Eskishehir, and Constantinople. The official claimed that only the lack of available railway transport kept him from sending off the children. The imminent danger was, however, far greater than it appeared. On 27 June the governor ordered Rohner to give up those orphans who were older than thirteen years and release all Armenian women from her staff. The orphans and women would be sent to Der Zor. The same day, Rössler reported that the local authorities were also deporting those Armenians who were longtime residents. The orders were executed ruthlessly.[137]

Despite strong police surveillance, the relief network continued to function and Rohner was able to forward information to Rössler and Constantinople. She requested funds for specific concentration camps once the opportunity arose for a courier to get there. Sometimes the couriers searched for deportees when relatives abroad contacted the German embassy inquiring about them or sent money.[138] The tireless relief effort could not, however, prevent the final stage in the extermination of Armenians along the Euphrates. On 29 July 1916 Rössler sent a summary report to Berlin. He had learned from a German official that the route along the river was covered with pieces of clothing. A local Ottoman military pharmacist had stated that about fifty-five thousand Armenians had been buried at Meskene alone. In the town of Der Zor, the authorities arrested all leading Armenians on 17 July, while on 22 July they began to deport all Armenians toward the desert.[139] Among the arrested and deported were Rohner's assistants. In her last letter to Rohner, Araxy Djebedjian, one of the volunteers, wrote: "Dear Sister. We cannot write to you any more. We are in great trouble, but thanks to God, we believe that He has the power to save us. Ah, is it not possible to do relief work with official permission from the authorities so that we can bring help to these miserable tents? I do not think at all of myself but the sight of those starving people is always before my eyes. As prisoners we are always very near death. If we do not see each other again here, we shall meet above." In her report to Constantinople, Rohner concluded: "Our beautiful work at Der Zor is at an end."[140]

Meanwhile at Aleppo, Rössler tried his best to induce the German and United States embassies to intervene on behalf of local Armenians. His aim was to prevent at least their deportation. The massacres north of Der Zor had also immediate consequences for the work of Rohner at Aleppo. The Ottoman authorities had tortured one of the arrested couriers and the victim had given up information about the work. Being compromised, Rohner gave up her role in the organization in order to avoid further danger to the general relief effort. She handed her work completely over to Consul Jackson.

The death of experienced staff and the increased danger to Armenian couriers motivated Jackson to enlist the support of August Bernau. Bernau was a German citizen working for the Vaccum Oil Company. In his professional capacity, he could create pretexts that necessitated traveling to the Lower Euphrates and thus reach the last concentration camps. In September 1916 Bernau reported that only about fifteen thousand Armenians were still alive along the Euphrates between Aleppo and the Der Zor district. The others had been massacred. Some of the few survivors who had escaped from the killing fields on the Khabur river managed to make their way back to Aleppo. Here they approached Rohner, who filed their depositions with the German consul. Thus, precise information on the actual implementation of the final extermination process became available to the German Foreign Office early on.[141]

The End of the Orphanage Work

Rohner's retreat from the general relief work came too late. The Ottoman authorities had evidently collected enough information on her work. In November 1916 they forced Rohner to submit a report on the founding and financing of her orphanage. Rohner conferred with Rössler. Both agreed to admit that the orphanage had received some subsidies from the German and United States consulates. Thus, Rohner avoided giving precise information. Rössler argued that a vaguer answer would only have resulted in further inquiries. In August 1916 Rohner had cared for 720 Armenians orphans. These children were the survivors of approximately 3,336 deportees. Thus, Rohner calculated the death rate at 78.5 percent until August 1916. The German embassy estimated total Armenian losses at 1,175,000 people up to that moment. Meanwhile, the authorities kept a close watch on Rohner's activities and made her orphanage work as difficult as possible. Any further relief work was absolutely out of the question under such circumstances. In view of the increasing political difficulties, Rohner tried to keep a delicate balance in trying to raise funds in neutral countries without compromising her work even more. Swiss relief organizations had published reports on the Genocide in the past that had attracted the attention of the Ottoman government. Now, Rohner offered to write appeals to important donors directly, thereby avoiding unwanted publicity. The funds were badly needed. By the end of December, the relief work immediately needed an extra 10,000 Turkish pounds to keep the work going, while the average weekly income stood at 5,000 pounds.[142]

Finally, in February 1917, the Ottoman government began to close down Rohner's orphanage. Djemal Pasha ordered that seventy boys should be taken from Aleppo to a new government orphanage in Lebanon. The Turkish nationalist activist Halideh Edib was in charge of this new institution. The government orphanage's main object was to assimilate the Armenian children. Of the remaining children, sixty were ill and could not be transported, while about 370 had escaped and gone into hiding. Since the government insisted on the delivery of four hundred orphans, the authorities took over other orphans who were being dressed and fed by Rohner. These orphans were sent to government orphanages in Konya, Balikesir, Ismid, and Adabazar. Parallel with the end of Rohner's orphanage, the government dissolved the local office of the IAMM. It seems that the government believed that the Armenians still surviving were no longer a major administrative issue. Despite all, the authorities invited Rohner to organize a new relief effort. The surviving Armenian women and children were either to work for the military workshops or to be placed in government orphanages. Rohner, however, left for Marash and later returned to Germany. She had suffered a nervous breakdown and it took her years to recover. In 1919 she published an appreciation, honoring her dead partners of the relief effort at Der Zor.[143]

Conclusion

In the spring of 1915, the Ottoman government began to exterminate the empire's Armenian population. The first bureaucratically organized genocide of the twentieth century had begun. Various government agencies oversaw and executed the crime. The state fully mobilized its civilian and military resources in order to render the genocidal program as efficient as possible. Thus, between May and September 1915, almost all Ottoman Armenians were deported for elimination or killed immediately. Only a handful of fragmented communities were left behind in Constantinople, Smyrna, and Aleppo. Most of the deportees who managed to escape from extermination or death through privation and disease in 1915 were deported again in the spring and summer of 1916. The vast majority of the survivors were killed in a series of massacres in the Syrian desert.

The international relief effort at Aleppo depended on a delicate balance. The German government was not willing to risk its good relations with its Ottoman ally over the fate of Armenians. For reasons of domestic politics, however, and in the interest of the German image abroad, the German Foreign Office was willing to support German humanitarian work to some extent. In a similar vein, the Ottoman central and local authorities appeared willing to accommodate German requests. The Ottoman government did not, however, cease to pursue its extermination program. Rohner's temporary permit for the running of her orphanage in no way contradicted the government's policy. In fact, she kept alive a large number of children who were later integrated into the authorities' assimilation program. Thus, Ottoman officials were willing to allow Rohner to do her part for this work. Her general relief work was, however, absolutely unacceptable for the Ottoman government. Her staff was persecuted and finally murdered. The considerable funds passing through the relief workers' hands were a constant temptation for the government to use for its own purposes. On the level of German-Ottoman relations, the permit given to Rohner provided an important element of excuse making for the Ottoman leaders. Like the German government, the Ottoman government needed something to demonstrate that the reports of massacres were untrue, at least in respect to the central government's involvement or intentions.

The United States' efforts stood in full contrast to the calculating attitudes of the German Foreign Office and its embassy at Constantinople. Ambassador Morgenthau and Consul Jackson stood out as examples of humanitarian consciousness and dedication. Thus, it was no surprise that the representatives of the United States took steps for the continuation of the work when United States– Ottoman relations were terminated and hostilities between the United States and Germany were about to begin in April 1917.[144] In combination with Swiss support, the cooperation between the ABCFM, the Hülfsbund, Jackson, and Rössler manifested a kind of humanitarian internationalism that confronted a genocidal regime against all odds. The situation was so desperate that Rössler went far beyond his official obligations. It seems safe to state that he probably went much farther than previously thought, although he avoided leaving traces.

Perhaps most surprising was that Beatrice Rohner, a woman, would take on the load of directing the relief effort at the most critical place at that time. She combined official and clandestine work under the threat of being court-martialed. German protection certainly provided some safety, and was crucial after the destruction of the relief network in the summer of 1916. Nevertheless, Rohner went beyond what was considered the proper conduct of a law-abiding citizen. She could rely on a number of self-sacrificing volunteers with whom she shared the same strong religious beliefs. The loss of her friend Eskijian was a first shock to her. The summary murder of many of her friends at the Khabour was a decisive setback. The final blow came when her orphans were taken away. She collapsed completely and had to leave the work she had built up despite all threats to her health and the constant danger posed by the local authorities.

It was the active resistance of the local Armenian communities and that of the deportees that made Rohner's efforts possible. While Armenians were victims, generally earmarked for death, they did not give up. At each stage on their deportation routes, Armenians organized some communal structure and thereby provided a base for relief workers. The orphanage work at Aleppo was a spontaneous creation of the local Armenian communities. Certainly, the available funds were insufficient in every respect, but the communities managed to demonstrate that something could still be done.

In his relief work, Reverend Eskijian had actively pursued several objects and strategies. He had understood that informing the outside world was essential for any attempt to stop the massacres of the deportees and to obtain enough funds to enable those who were still alive to survive. Consequently, for extended periods of time, he and his collaborators underwent considerable risks to inform United States consul Jackson on the unfolding genocide.

Gulenia Eskijian, 1945

It is safe to assume that they also used the services of Beatrice Rohner to inform the German consul. Eskijian built up an initial relief network that provided the first help to deportees in Aleppo. Moreover, he understood that the situation of the deportees in the desert and outlying places was much worse. Thus, he managed to organize a network of volunteers who served as messengers between the concentration camps and the center of the relief effort at Aleppo. The international relief effort could therefore depend on an already established organization for its distribution of relief funds from abroad. Indeed, any international relief depended fully on these networks as few foreigners were able to travel to Aleppo and even fewer managed to travel into the desert regions where the mass murders reached their final climax.

Eskijian was realistic enough to see that he could not save all deportees. In response to the lack of resources, he pooled the limited funds he had at hand and concentrated the relief work on a selected group of people. Intellectuals, orphans, and teenagers were the Ottoman government's prime targets earmarked for destruction. They also were Eskijian's prime candidates for salvation. These young people would be the next generation who would raise families and secure a continued Armenian existence in the Middle East. Eskijian also understood that the protection of intellectuals, priests, and other professionals was crucial for the survival of any meaningful Armenian identity—be it cultural, political, or economic. In sum, his relief effort was a program for national survival against all odds. Evidently, the reverend had fully understood the intentions of the Ottoman rulers and put up resistance against their program as well as he could.

Eskijian was not a calculating man. He was deeply compassionate and gave literally all he had. Sharing his last piece of bread was not an empty word in his house, which he had turned into a shelter for the persecuted. It is doubtful, however, that he could have done what he did without the support of his wife, Gulenia. Most likely for cultural reasons, she kept a rather low profile and did not act publicly. However, in matters concerning orphan girls, she assumed a leadership role. Being familiar with the secrets of the underground network, she was the one person who could secure the continuation of the relief work after her husband's death. It is difficult to imagine what it meant to her to be left alone with two small children, being threatened herself by the constant danger of police raids, and facing an overwhelming task in front of her. There was possibly little time for mourning. Nevertheless, she assumed the role that had fallen to her and continued the work as long as possible. However, she had to cope with the increasing repression of relief work by the local authorities. One helper after another was arrested and disappeared, never to return again. Asking volunteers to take up the work became almost a request to accept a death sentence. But not only the volunteers faced death; more and more orphans were taken away by the police in order to be assimilated, to be killed, or to become sex slaves for the Turkish elite. In the end, a small group of remaining children found shelter with Rohner, and the work was disbanded. It was certainly consoling to Mrs. Eskijian that some of the volunteers managed to survive. They contacted the widow and her children in later years and kept the memory of Hovhannes Eskijian alive.

In the final analysis, the relief effort had no chance in altering the Ottoman government's determination to exterminate the empire's Armenian population. The humanitarian resistance had no tools to stop massacres and put an end to the bloodbath. However, a comparatively large number of the children who had been sheltered in the orphanages of Aleppo survived the war and became part of the emerging Armenian communities in exile later on. In 1918 Bertha Morley took over the orphanage in Lebanon where some of the Aleppo orphans who had been singled out for assimilation by Halideh Edib were staying.[145] Together with those who survived in the underground and the few who survived thanks to a protected status, these Armenians built new communities in exile after World War I. A return to their homeland was out of the question. The newly declared Republic of Turkey continued to persecute Armenians. This was no surprise, since the chief organizers of the Armenian Genocide were leading among the founders of the new state.

The Man He Was
by Nancy Eskijian

"He rests from his labors and his works do follow him."
Revelation 14:13.

Rev. Eskijian perished in a sacrificial effort to save Armenians marked for extermination by the Turkish government in the Genocide of 1915. Some men run when they hear the cries of people, others hear the voice of God. Rev. Eskijian was one such person.

As he said in one of his messages as the dark clouds of war and Genocide fell on Aleppo: "Dear friends, be courageous. Let us die, but let no one deny his Lord. This honorable opportunity does not come to us often. I myself am ready for the gallows."[1]

His message would turn out to be prophetic. After depleting and exhausting himself to save as many as he could, he died in a hospital bed of typhus, which he presumably caught from the lice on the orphans he embraced. He died the day before he was to be publicly hanged.[2] He had been warned several times by Turkish authorities to stop his humanitarian mission regarding incoming Armenian refugees. But he challenged that brutal order according to Bible truth: Obey God rather than men. Acts 5:29.[3]

It is reported that when the gendarmes came to take him away from his hospital bed to be hanged, Mrs. Eskijian said, you can't have him, he's free.

And he always was a free man—free to do the will of His Father in heaven, free to obey a higher call. His final words to his wife were: "I am thankful. Praise His name forever. It does not matter— whether I live or die. There is no death for me. Love to all."[4] Hundreds attended his funeral, a nation mourned, and his memory lives on.

Rev. Eskijian was born on February 23, 1982 in Ourfa, Turkey, and died in 1916 at the age of 34 in Aleppo, Syria. The last of 11 children, of which only 3 survived, he was well-loved, a beautiful child, the son of a shoe repairman, "Eskiji," as the name depicted.

When he was 7 years old, he became very sick and the best doctors could not help. Saying he only had a few days to live, his mother would not accept the doctor's verdict, and said, wait, you will see. She fasted for 40 days, praying the crying, "O Lord, please save my son's life. I dedicate him to you."[5] He lived and his life was spent in the service of the His Lord.

In 1895 the Turks entered his family home and killed his father with a sledge hammer, and then beheaded him, as his mother watched. They dragged him through the streets, dumping him in a common grave. At that time many other Armenians were burned in the Ourfa church where they fled for sanctuary. Hovhannes Eskijian and his brother were hiding in an open tomb. This was the second time his life was spared. He acknowledged that the Lord had a special reason to save his life.[6]

So, at an early age became an orphan himself. As it would turn out, his own loss simply became preparation for the special ministry ahead. He spent the next few years in the American orphanage mentored by Miss Corrine Shattuck where he was encouraged in the Christian faith. He transferred to Aintab Boys College. Miss Shattuck recognized the Hovhannes had a very promising future, paying all expenses for his education. In due time he gave his life to Christ. Miss Shattuck knew his call was preacher and she asked him if he wanted to become a minister. His answer was, 'knowing God's love and tasting the Lord's sweetness, how can I deny this great news and preach to others. That love has forced me to become a preacher.' On June 15, 1905, he graduated from Aintab Boys College. He attained the top of his class, giving the valedictorian speech.[7]

Miss Shattuck also paid for his advanced education at Marash Theological Seminary. After two years of successful study, he graduated in June 1908, and started preaching at the age of 26 in local villages.[8]

Hovhannes finished seminary in 1908. About that time he met Miss Gulenia Danielian, a graduate of the Marash Girls College and a teacher. Her prayer was to find someone who would do the Lord's work and will, so that she could put her education and Christian service together. "God answered my prayers. But my family and friends all said no, because we were wealthy and Rev. Eskijian had nothing, but we both insisted. When they saw our sincere desire, God softened their hearts and everyone agreed. On July 14, 1910 they were married. "The first thing we did, as soon as we were married, we both came to our knees in the Lord's holy presence, making the pledge to the Lord that we will serve the Lord with all our hearts, soul and body, in our entire lives."[9]

Their lives would soon be thrown into utmost sacrifice in the maelstrom of the Genocide. Later in 1910 Rev. Eskijian began to pastor the churches of the tiny villages near Kessab, Syria, Ekiz-Oluk, Keurkune and Kaladouran. In the next three years the couple had two children, John and Luther. But in 1913 they were called to pastor the Armenian Evangelical Church of Aleppo at a critical time—God's hand, God's timing. "Without any doubt, it was the providential arrangement of God that Rev. and Mrs. Eskijian were transferred in 1913 from the pastorate in Ekiz-Oluk, Keurkune and Kaladouran to a pastorate in Aleppo. God was confident that this young couple through their spirit of service and sacrifice with direct guidance form God, would be the means of salvation to hundreds of Armenians, young and old, orphans and widows, from the fiendish torture, humiliation and death by Turkish hordes. At this critical time, Rev. and Mrs. Eskijian gave many suffering Armenians food, service, shelter in their home and orphanage or provided hiding places to those being hunted by the Turks."[10] "Rev. Eskijian truly was a great Christian. The secret of his fearless work was his private and intimate communication with the Lord. He was a believer in the power of prayer. Every day he prayed for the salvation of his people before leaving his house."[11]

"The days were full of sorrow and suffering. The Armenian nation was being departed by force to the slaughterhouses in the deserts. The total atmosphere was cruelty, suffering, and death by torture. During those days of calamity, the Armenian nation needed a leader of exceptional abilities, fearlessness, and self sacrifice, who knew his own power and capabilities, and was ready to put all his abilities in the service of the nation. That exceptional person was Rev. Hovhannes Eskijian. He was a God-sent angel, only without wings. This angel of God suffered terribly when he saw the extreme suffering of his nation which was being consumed by the flames of destruction erupting from men like Enver and Talaat. One of Rev. Eskijian's services was the establishment of an orphanage in Aleppo. I myself miraculously saved from several bloody deaths, was received in this orphanage as a boy of 16, and was saved both in body and spirit. Rev. Eskijian was my savior in Body, and Christ saved my soul in the same orphanage.... I still remember the fatherly visits of Rev. Eskijian, who often gathered us around him and prayed for us and with us."[12]

So it started: "The deportations of 1915 opened vast avenues of service before Rev. Eskijian. Aleppo was the crossroads on the highway of deportation. Thousands of Armenians were brought in to be deported to the slaughter houses of Der Zor, Ras ul Ain, Sheddade and elsewhere to die of starvation and fatigue. The vast khans and factories of Aleppo were filled with refugees and emptied to be filled again by newcomers, persecuted, half-naked and starving. Rev. and Mrs. Eskijian were busy every day with these people. Not only did they welcome many of these Armenians into their own home, but also served them outside their home in many hiding places. They administered food, medicine, money and protection to their utmost capacity."

He obtained financial assistance from different sources, including the American Embassy in Aleppo which was transmitted to the needy with Father Harutune Yayian of the Armenian Apostolic Diocese.

He found employment for many boys, girls and young women as servants in different Arab families. His motto was, "We must do all we can do to save one more Armenian by all possible means."

He found employment for many young Armenians with the German Railroad Company, opening tunnels for the Berlin-Baghdad railway in the Amanos mountains near Entelly.

The more dangerous the situation the more energetic and courageous he became.

He sent quinine and financial assistance to Armenian refugees in Hama, Homs, Damascus, Hauran, even Der Zor, Meskene, Ras ul Ain. His agents were Armenians disguised as Arabs who talked Arabic. He had many co-workers who had contacts with Arab and Turkish officials and Arab drivers and muleteers. One of his important helpers was a chief police officer, by the Selim Effendi, an Albanian by origin. He himself defended many families hidden in and around the Armenian Evangelical Church. Whenever there was a plan for official investigation of the refugees, he informed Rev. Eskijian a day ahead of time, so that he could change the hiding places.

During the months when Protestant Armenians were immune from deportation, Rev. Eskijian used that opportunity to its fullest capacity. (He would go through the trains passing through Aleppo, and pick up the children, young women and men—whether Protestant or non-Protestant and bring them into town.)[13]

Rev. Eskijian had a great plan and studied many possibilities. It entailed the transfer of many Armenians from the Deir el Zor and Ras ul Ain areas, to some safe place in the Dersim area where friendly Kurds lived.... He had a great plan and studied many possibilities to help his people, but his unexpected death left many plans unfulfilled."[14]

He corresponded with the Mr. Jesse Jackson, the charge de affairs of the American Embassy to alleviate the suffering to the Armenians and tell the world. "Rev. Eskijian, disregarding the safety of his life, filled the American Embassy with secret reports and bulletins so that after his formal petition, Mr. Jackson, and the U.S. Ambassador informed in detail all the events of the day to his government. Soon after that came the big moment of organized relief...thousands and thousands of lives were saved by his letter relief work."[15]

The following is summarized from the compilation of M. H. Shnorhokian:

In 1915 Armenians poured into Aleppo setting up makeshift tents, perhaps their last homes, amid filth, lice, corpses, and starving, sick people waiting to be sent to the desert. At two notorious deportation centers Karlik and the Railway Station in Aleppo, Rev. Eskijian helped destitute Armenians. Rev. Eskijian would find hundreds of these desperate Armenians and save them from the death marches.

He had a special passport to enter these death stations and give help to the Armenians, which permit he utilized to the fullest. Giving up sleep, he listened for the sounds of the trains and headed to the stations. He went through the wagons and picked up the children, young girls and young men and brought them into town.

From a testimony of Rahel Megerdichian: Rev. Eskijian would also go to Karlik at night, picking up Armenian orphans, bringing them to his home under his coat. Mrs. Eskijian washed, clothed and fed them. He had agents who helped many Armenians to escape from Karlik, personally making a trip there to save Mrs. Megerdichian's brother.[16]

The refugees came all day from morning to evening. Mrs. Eskijian ministered to their physical needs. Rev. Eskijian tried to find shelter, clothes and food, and maintained contact with those in hiding. By Rev. E. Elmajian: "While in their home, Rev. and Mrs. Eskijian did for me all that one's own parents would do. In addition to all of their home duties and care of her two little children, Emmanuel and Luther, Mrs. Eskijian left none of my needs unattended. I cannot forget the sacrificial service I received from her. She also served with unexcelled devotion to the daily increasing number of Armenian refugees who came to her for needed help. I cannot fully describe the pitiful condition of the refugees who used to come all day, form early morning to late evening for urgent help which overtaxed Mrs. Eskijian beyond the limit of her physical endurance.... What I witnessed during the period of three months I stayed in Rev. Eskijian's home is too heartbreaking to describe. He had to do something with the children who had lost their parents. He had to listen to the pathetic stories of women, how their husbands were tortured and murdered before their eyes, how they were forced by Turkish gendarmes to walk many miles day after day, barefooted, without sufficient food and clothing, and without being allowed to drink water when water was available; how so many young girls among them were molested and others taken into Turkish harems. His sympathetic heart used to melt by listening to numerous such heart crushing experiences which were too hard on his nerves. He could not rest without providing some sort of temporary physical rest and spiritual comfort for their bleeding heart with a message from the scriptures to place their trust in God."[17]

He opened an orphanage for the children, roaming through the streets of the city, and taking these young ones to be saved. When one young man complained that Rev. Eskijian had not saved his parents, he replied that the young must be saved so that the nation would not perish.

***

John Minassian, his young assistant, estimated that thousands of Armenians were saved from death by his efforts, and the efforts of those who joined him in this endeavor.[18] Some called him the "white angel" and the people he ministered to, loved him as their own fathers and mothers, and grieved just as deeply when he died.

The kind of man he was: Rev. Eskijian's acts were only a reflection of his deeply committed faith in the Lord Jesus Christ. One cannot separate the acts from the treasures of the man's heart, the truth that transformed him and then conformed him to the image of Jesus Christ.

Jesus said: "Whosoever will come after Me, let him deny himself and take up his cross, and follow Me. For whosoever will save his life shall lose it, but whosoever shall lose his life for My sake and the gospel's, the same shall save it." Mark 8:34-35 Rev. Eskijian took these words of Jesus seriously, and walked wherever the Lord said, Go.

Like Paul, Rev. Eskijian could say, "For me to live is Christ and to die is gain." Philippians 1:21. As recounted in a letter by Mrs. Yevnigi Jebijian: "When he gave me the news of my brother, Rev. Koundakjian's, death, he was very calm." He said, "Dickran's death was necessary for the cause." He could see his own death. He told me sincerely one day, "if the Lord wants one person to be sacrificed to save His people, with all my heart, I want to be that person."[19]

"Lay not up for yourselves treasures on earth where moth and rust corrupt and thieves break through and steal, but lay up for yourselves treasures in heaven. Each saved life was a treasure stored up in heaven for Rev. Eskijian.

"From an article by Rev. Elmajian who was assisted at his orphanage as a young man: "He was a patient, humble, affectionate man. All day long to everyone, good or bad, had a sweet word of comfort, with an angelic smile without hurting anyone. I used to watch this holy man who had a treasure in his heart to everyone. I never saw anger, impatience or complaint at any time. In his orphanage which he started, miraculously saving the poor orphans from the hand of Turks, he had no rest day or night. He forgot his home and sleep. Rev. Eskijian had not only saved Protestants, but whoever came to him Gregorian or Catholic. He helped them all and he never forced anyone to become a Protestant in order to give help. He never held back any money when it came to save somebody's life. In his weak physical condition, he carried a heart of a lion. He never put his own life first. He was not afraid of dying. He spent time with the sick, carrying them, helping them, until he finally got the same typhus that they were carrying. Even with typhus in his body he did not stop working. When he died the whole nation cried for him. Everybody thought now they were really orphans."[20]

"As I said...he never got tired or disgusted. Such things would have been disloyalty for him.... For the big men, beyond the light there is the summit.... Fortunately I have been one of those who saw him on the summit. Most often he left his pulpit empty to pay his habitual visits to the sick and unfortunate. He took their tiny, cold hands in his own hands to warm them and their despaired life, comforting with his warm breath. After the setting of Rev. Eskijian's sun, all those stars who tried to illuminate the darkness around them, were mere candle light. Our Lord Jesus Christ was glorified through the Badvily."[21]

Rev. Hovhannes Eskijian himself was one of those stars rendering divers services in the camps of the unfortunate deported refugees in Aleppo City, Syria. All his activities there were so unparalleled and unique that his unselfish and sacrificial life was admired of the old and experienced pastors, adorning the young pastor's forehead as if with a golden crown. Rev. Eskijian was a sincere and earnest believer. Many times I have had private prayers with him and found out the source of his heroic strength.

His faith was based on the cross; his desires, thoughts and actions were benevolent and patriotic. He had the highest ideal, which was evident that he was reaching out towards that very purpose.

In those dark and hopeless days, his sermons were hope inspiring. Like a prophet he used the events and messages of the Bible as a balm upon broken hearts and divine promises as solace. He used to encourage and cheer with the message of resurrection those who were facing death and the grave. He strengthened those undying souls and served the faith and hope of those who had submerged in the slough of despondence.[22]

Jesus tells us: "Verily, verily I say unto you, unless a corn of wheat falls to the ground and die, it abides alone, but if it die, it brings forth much fruit. He that loveth his life shall lose it and he that hateth his life in this world shall keep it unto life eternal. If any man serve Me, let him follow Me and where I am there shall also My servant be: if any man serve Me, him will My Father honor." John 12:24-26. The words could not summarize more completely the life of Rev. Eskijian. He sacrificed himself, and that sacrifice bore much fruit. He put aside his life in this world to procure eternal life for himself and others. And wherever His Master went, there the servant went also. Today and for eternity, the man who served Him will be honored of the Father.

Of his death John Minassian said this: "Without being driven by fanatic sentiments, I would like to add this: that when I approached his coffin, I saw a glorious and splendid form on his face. Although he was in the hands of death, yet had won the battle. He had kept his usual smile, which meant to say to me and all: I have fought the good fight and I have finished the race, I have kept the faith. II Tim 4:7. Whatever was given to me, I am returning it back to you with big interest."[23]

Of his funeral his wife wrote to her sister: "Oh dear, you should have seen that mournful, yet very much exalted spectacle. Everybody, old and young, Armenians and non-Armenians, wept bitterly. Hundreds and hundreds tried for the last time to show their love and respect to the forever departed 'Badvely' their protector. Thanks to our Almighty Father who is in heaven, and the nation, and everybody, who participated for the last time in this sad event."

John Minassian at his funeral: "Do you think we are going to forget you because you are no more? And because we do not see your cheerful face and do not hear your honey sweet words from your life? No, never, far be that ungrateful thought. You, who became father for the orphans, a comforter for the widows, shadow and help to the needy and much loved by multitudes.

We will never forget you. Instead we will follow your example and bless you forever."[25]

Mrs. Victoria Shnorhokian in remembering the following quotation from Rev. Eskijian: "There are Christians who live one and speak ten. There are also Christians who live ten and speak one. We should be Christians of this second type." Rev. Eskijian himself belonged to the latter class.[26]

On his gravestone (which had been desecrated several times): "Rev. Hovhannes Eskijian, Called to Higher Service, March 25, 1916. 'His servants shall serve Him and shall see his face.' Revelations 22:24."

A poem written to him: "This servant's work is done, the labor here is changed for the service of a holier sphere, and he, the servant to the Master gone to count the gathered gain, the conflicts won. Here with the Lord unseen the way he trod. Translated here he sees and walks with God, Here are the lower fields while he wrought, But God has taken him and he is not."

Well done thou good and faithful servant,... enter into the joy of the Lord. Matthew 25:21.

Endnotes for pages 1-59

1. On the murder of a local official who did not execute the orders of the central government see: Nesimi, Abidin, *Yýllarýn Ýçinden*, Istanbul: Gözlem Yayýnlarý, 1978, pp.40-46.

2. On German propaganda and genocide denial during World War I see: Hilmar Kaiser, "Le génocide arménien: négation 'à l'allemande'" *L'actualité du Génocide des Arméniens. Actes du colloque organisé par le Comité de Défense de la Cause Arménienne*, (Preface by Jack Lang), Paris: Edipol, 1999, pp.75-91.

3. James L. Barton *Story of Near East Relief (1915-1930). An Interpretation*, New York, NY: Macmillan, 1930.

4. Ulrich Trumpener, *Germany and the Ottoman Empire, 1914 - 1918*, Princeton, NJ: Princeton University Press, 1968; reprint, Delmar, NY: Caravan Books, 1989); Frank G. Weber, *Eagles on the Crescent. Germany, Austria and the Diplomacy of the Turkish Alliance, 1914-1918*, Ithaca, Cornell University Press, 1970; W.E.D. Allen / Paul Muratoff, *Caucasian Battlefields. A History of the Wars on the Turco-Caucasian Border, 1828-1921*, Cambridge: Cambridge University Press, 1953; Wilhelm Litten, *Persische Flitterwochen*, Berlin: Georg Stilke, 1925; Hans Lührs, *Der Gegenspieler des Obersten Lawrence*, Berlin: Otto Schlegel, 1936; Friedrich Kress von Kressenstein, *Mit den Türken zum Suezkanal. Erinnerungen eines deutschen Generalstabsoffiziers in türkischen Diensten*, Berlin: Vorhut-Verlag, 1938. The recent study of Erickson on the Ottoman army is based almost entirely on official Turkish war histories. The accounts of German commanders in the Ottoman army, German and Austrian studies, as well as the rich Turkish memoir literature were left out of consideration with only minor exceptions. Thus, the study is not much more than a short summary of the official war histories. Edward J. Erickson, *Ordered to Die. A History of the Ottoman in the First World War*, Westport, CT: The Greenwood Press (Contributions in Military Studies, no. 201) 2001.

5. Carl Mühlmann, *Oberste Heeresleitung und Balkan im Weltkrieg 1914/1918*, Berlin: Wilhelm Limpert Verlag, 1942 pp.80-81.

6. On the defense of Van see: Anahide Ter Minassian, "Van 1915" in Richard G. Hovannisian (ed.), *Armenian Van/Vaspurakan*, Costa Mesa, CA: Mazda Publishers (UCLA Armenian History and Culture Series, Historic Armenian Cities and Provinces, 1) 2000, pp. 209-244.

7.   See the memoirs of a leading Ottoman officer in Djemal's staff: Ali
        Fuad Erden, *Birinci Dünya Harbinde Suriye Hâtýralarý*, vol. 1, Istanbul:
        Halk Matbaasý, 1954 pp.115-116 (all published). His account is con-
        firmed by Djemal's own memoirs, written after the war in Germany.
        Cemal Paþa, *Hâtýralar*, (ed. by Behçet Cemal), Istanbul: Selek Yayýn-
        larý, 1959 p.360. A German serving in the Ottoman army was in charge
        of the mobilization against Zeitoun. He recorded his impressions and
        reasonings in his letters to his wife and father. Eberhard Wolffskeel
        von Reichenberg, *Zeitoun, Mousa Dagh, Ourfa. Letters on the Armenian
        Genocide*, (ed. and intro. by Hilmar Kaiser), Princeton, NJ: Gomidas In-
        stitute, 2001 pp.3-15. For Djemal's motives in regard to the inhabitant's
        deportation see: Djemal to Enver, Jerusalem, April 10, 1915 telegram
        3108 in: *Documents*, [Ankara]; Prime Ministry, Directorate General of
        Press and Information, n.d. The book is a translation of Askeri Tarih
        Belgeleri Dergisi 81 (1982) pp.52-53. On the initial phase of the depor-
        tations in the Zeitoun region see Djemal to Enver, Damascus, April 5,
        1915 No. 3023 in, *Askeri Tarih Belgeleri Dergisi* 86 (1987) pp.24-26.

8.   For a discussion of the events leading up to the arrests of April 24,
        1915, and the immediate aftermath see: Hilmar Kaiser, "The Arme-
        nian Genocide: Governing Myths Revisited," paper presented at the
        'Second Mediterranean Social and Political Research Meeting' Europe-
        an University Institute, Florence, March 21–25, 2001 (forthcoming). In
        her recent study on Komitas Vartabed Rita Soulahian Kuyumjian gave
        an extensive and detailed summary of Aram Andonian's memoirs on
        his arrest and subsequent deportation from Constantinople to Chan-
        giri. The material had appeared originally in 1947 in an Armenian
        language daily in Paris. Rita Soulahian Kuyumjian, *Archeology of Mad-
        ness. Komitas, Portrait of an Icon*, Princeton, N.J.; Gomidas Institute, 2001
        pp.116-134.

9.   Erden, *Suriye Hâtýralarý*, p.116, 121-122. It is important to note that most
        of these early deportees from the Cilician region were deported to
        areas in southern Syria or allowed to remain in the vicinity to Aleppo.
        Thus, the survival rate among these deportees was considerably higher
        than those among later deportees. Erden claims that the comparably
        better treatment of Armenian deportees in areas controlled by Djemal
        Pasha aroused the anger of Behaeddin Shakir.

10.   For the text of the memorandum see Beylerian, Arthur (ed.), *Les
        grandes puissances, l'Empire ottoman et les Arméniens dans les archives français-*

es (1914-1918). Recueil de documents, Paris: Publications de la Sorbonne (Série Documents, 34), 1983 p.29 (doc. 41).

11. For information on deportations in various regions see the eye-witness accounts published in: James Bryce / Arnold Toynbee, *The Treatment of Armenians in the Ottoman Empire, 1915-1916: Documents Presented to Viscount Grey of Fallodon by Viscount Bryce* [Uncensored Edition], (ed. and intro. by Ara Sarafian), Princeton, NJ: Gomidas Institute, 2000. The book was published first in 1916. On the various manuals and the confiscation program see: Hilmar Kaiser, "Armenian Property, Ottoman Law, and Nationality Policies During the Armenian Genocide, 1915-1915," paper presented at the International Workshop Ethnic Conflict and the Founding of the Turkish Republic, Rijksuniversiteit Leiden, May 17, 2000 (forthcoming). The Ottoman government's demographic policies and the role of deportations and confiscations in this context are discussed in: Fikret Adanýr / Hilmar Kaiser, "Migration, Deportation, and Nation-Building: the Case of the Ottoman Empire" in René Leboutte (ed.), *Migrations and Migrants in Historical Perspective. Permanencies and Innovations*, Bruxelles: Peter Lang, 2000 pp.273-292.

12. For a discussion of deportations from the western provinces, see: Hilmar Kaiser," The Baghdad Railway and the Armenian Genocide, 1915-1916: A Case Study in German Resistance and Complicity" Richard G. Hovannisian (ed.), *Remembrance and Denial: The Case of the Armenian Genocide*, Detroit: Wayne State University Press, 1998 pp.67-112.

13. Elise Hagobian-Taft, *Rebirth. The Story of an Armenian Girl Who Survived the Genocide and Found Rebirth in America*, Plandome, N.Y.: New Age Publishers, 1981 p.40.

14. Ibid., p.41.

15. "Beaucoup de gens disent: "Voilà, *aux protestants et aux grégoriens arririvent dès secours de Constantinople par le moyen de leurs Patriarcats,* et nous nous avons un grand Pape, son digne Délégué Mons. Dolci, nous avons notre vénéré Patriarche et son Saint Vicaire, comme aussi S.G. Mgr. Sayegh, nous avons les prêtres et des Pères compatriotes ou non, pourquoi tous ceux-ci ne pensent-ils pas à nous; si l'argent leur manque, il y a tant de catholiques, en commençant par l'Ambassadeur d'Autriche. S.E. Mr Pallavicini; pourquoi ne font-ils pas recour à ces personnages, ne les implorent ne sauver?" Telles sont leur paroles ils disent qu'ils disent qu'ils ont offert leurs personnes pour la gloire de l'église et ils disent qu'ils cherchent un Pasteur courageus qui se sacrifià à ses

ouailles." Kazezian to Armenian Catholic Patriarchate, Konia, November 22, 1915 Archivio Segreto Vaticano (ASV), Archivio Delegazione Apostolica in Turchia, Carte Mons. Dolci, Busta 8. Dolci to Gasparri, Constantinople, December 12, 1915 (12687) No. 114 Archivio della sacra congregazione degli affari ecclesiastici straordinari, Vatican, Austria 463. Sabatino to Dolci, Aleppo, November 7, 1916 ASV, Archivio Delegazione Apostolica in Turchia, Carte Mons. Dolci, Busta 9, Atti della Delegazione Apostolica di Costantinopoli 1916. Kaiser, *Baghdad Railway*, p. 78. On the policies of the Holy See during the Armenian Genocide see: Andrea Riccardi, *Il Mediterraneo. Cristianesimo e islam tra coabitazione e conflitto*, Milano: Guerini e Associati, 1997 pp.101-145.

16.   On the massacres in the plain of Moush see: Anahide Ter Minassian, "Un exemple, Mouch 1915" *L'actualité du Génocide des Arméniens*, pp.231-252.

17.   Henry H. Riggs, *Days of Tragedy in Armenia. Personal Experiences in Harpoot, 1915-1917*, Ann Arbor, MI: Gomidas Institute, 1997. Numerous survivors have left their accounts of the deportation and the massacres. For a comprehensive study of survivors' experiences see: Donald E. Miller / Lorna Touryan Miller, *An Oral History of the Armenian Genocide,* Berkeley: California University Press, 1993.

18.   For information on the massacres of deportees in the valleys along the Euphrates river see: ASV, Archivio Delegazione Apostolica in Turchia, Carte Mons. Dolci, Busta 5, Incidents de Malatia. Racconté par un temoin oculaire, June 1915, copy. Bryce/Toynbee, *Treatment*, pp.276-283; Riggs, *Days of Tragedy*. On the massacres and concentration camps in the Syrian desert see, Kévorkian, Raymond, "Le sort des déportés dans les camps de concentration de Syrie et de Mésopotamie," *Revue d'histoire arménienne contemporaine*, 2 (1998) pp.7-61; Idem, "Témoignages sur les camps de concentration de Syrie et de Mésopotamie," Ibid., 62-215; Idem, "Autres témoignages sur les déportations et les camps de concentration de Syrie et de Mésopotamie (1915-1916)," Ibid., 219-244; Auswärtiges Amt – Politisches Archiv, Berlin (hereafter: AA-PA), Anonymous, "The Migration of the Armenians to Deir Zor," Aleppo, November 11, 1915, enclosure in Rössler to Bethmann Hollweg, Aleppo, November 16, 1915 A 35047 AA-PA Türkei 183/40No. 2078.

19.   Litten, *Flitterwochen,* pp.304-310.

20.   Kaiser, *Baghdad Railway*.

21. Rössler to Embassy, Aleppo, March 12, 1915 J. No. 1516 AA-PA Konstantinopel 168 telegram; Rössler to Embassy, Aleppo, March 25, 1915 J. No. 1860 Ibid. telegram; Rössler to Embassy, Aleppo, March 26, 1915 J. No. 1886 Ibid. telegram; Rössler to Embassy, Marash, Mar. 31, 1915 Ibid. telegram; Rössler to Embassy, Marash, April 2, 1915 J. No. 2050 Ibid. telegram; Rössler to Wangenheim, Aleppo, April 12, 1915 A 14801 AA-PA Türkei 183/36 No.764.

22. Wolffskeel, *Zeitoun, Mousa Dagh, Ourfa*, pp.xiv, 3-15.

23. Jackson to Morgenthau, Aleppo, June 5, 1915 US-NA Record Group 59. 867.4016/77 No. 289 in, Ara Sarafian (compiler),), *United States Official Documents on the Armenian Genocide*, Vol. 1, Watertown, MA: Armenian Review (Archival Collections on the Armenian Genocide), 1993 pp.18-20. An American missionary, Alice Shepard Riggs, recalled Djelal's humane attitudes toward the Armenians: "When the wave of deportation had reached, and swept over, the neighboring towns and was theatening Aintab, Dr. Shepard made a strong appeal to the *Vali* [Governor General] of the province of Aleppo, and this official, who was a righteous man, firmly prevented the action being carried out." Alice Shepard Riggs, *Shepard of Aintab*, New York, N.Y.: Interchurch Press, 1920 p.190. See also Kévorkian, *Témoignages*, p.99. Aram Andonian, *Documents officiels concernant les massacres arméniens*, translated by S. David-Beg, Paris: Imprimerie H. Turabian, 1920 p.27.

24. For a discusssion of the department's work see: Kaiser, *Armenian Property*. On the Eyoub Bey see: Ipek, Nedim, "Birinci Dünya Savaþ Esnasýnda Karadeniz ve Doðu-Anadolu'da Cereyan Eden Göçler" *19 Mayis ve Milli Mücadelede Samsun Sempozyumu*, Bildiriler, 16-20 Mayis 1994, Samsun, n.p., n.d., pp.75-77.

25. Rössler to Embassy, Aleppo, May 3, 1915 J. No. 2687 AA-PA Konstantinopel 168 telegram; Rössler to Embassy, Aleppo, June 6, 1915 J. No. 3451 AA-PA Konstantinopel 169 telegram; Rössler to Embassy, Aleppo, June 12, 1915 J. No. 3594 AA-PA Konstantinopel 169 telegram.

26. Rössler to Wangenheim, Aleppo, June 19, 1915 J. No. 4981 AA-PA Konstantinopel 96 no.1288.

27. Rössler to Embassy, Aleppo, June 21, 1915 J. No. 3790 AA-PA Konstantinopel 169 telegram 9; Rössler to Embassy, Aleppo, June 21, 1915 J. No. 3799 AA-PA Konstantinopel 169 telegram 10. On June 28, Dje-

lal Bey had lost his post at Aleppo and left the city early in July for Constantinople. Rössler to Embassy, Aleppo, June 28, 1915 J. No. 1366 AA-PA Konsulat Aleppo, Pkt. 1 Bd.1/2 telegram 18; Rössler to Embassy, Aleppo, July 5, 1915 J. No. 1437 AA-PA Konsulat Aleppo, Pkt. 1 Bd.1/2 telegram 33; Rössler to Bethmann Hollweg, Aleppo, June 29, 1915 A 22125 AA-PA Türkei 183/37 No.1382.

28. Rössler to Embassy, Aleppo, June 29, 1915 J. No. 3967 AA-PA Konstantinopel 169 telegram 20; Rössler to Embassy, Aleppo, July 8, 1915 J. No. 4141 AA-PA Konstantinopel 169 telegram 35; Rössler to Bethmann Hollweg, Aleppo, July 17, 1915 A 23232 AA-PA Türkei 183/37 No.1553; Rössler to Bethmann Hollweg, Aleppo, July 27, 1915 A 23991 AA-PA Türkei 183/38 No. 1645.

29. Rössler to Embassy, Aleppo, July 27, 1915 J. No. 4414 AA-PA Konstantinopel 170 telegram 50; Rössler to Bethmann Hollweg, Aleppo, July 27, 1915 A 23991 AA-PA Türkei 183/38 No. 1645; Rössler to Embassy, Aleppo, July 30, 1915 J. No. 4453 AA-PA Konstantinopel 170 telegram 53; Rössler to Embassy, Aleppo, August 1, 1915 J. No. 6255 AA-PA Konstantinopel 96; Rössler to Bethmann Hollweg, Aleppo, July 31, 1915 A 24524 AA-PA Türkei 183/38 No.1665.

30. Jackson to Morgenthau, Aleppo, August 3, 1915 US-NA Record Group 59. 867.4016/129 No. 333 in, Sarafian (compiler), *United States Official Documents*, pp.39-41.

31. Baþbakanlýk Osmanlý Arþivi, Dâhiliye Nezâreti Evraký, Dâhiliye Þifre Kalemi (hereafter: DH. ÞFR), Ministry to Aleppo province, Constantinople, July 22, 1915 EUM BOA.DH.ÞFR 54a/71; Talaat to Zor district, Constantinople, July 24, 1916 EUM Special 28 Ibid. 54a/91.

32. Rössler to Embassy, Aleppo, August 3, 1915 J. No. 4517 AA-PA Konstantinopel 170 telegram 56; Rössler to Embassy, Aleppo, August 7, 1915 J. No. 4575 AA-PA Konstantinopel 169 telegram 63; Rössler to Embassy, Aleppo, August 12, 1915 J. No. 4683 AA-PA Konstantinopel 170 telegram 69; Rössler to Bethmann Hollweg, Aleppo, August 13, 1915 A 25860 AA-PA Türkei 183/38 No. 1772.

33. Rössler to Embassy, Aleppo, August 15, 1915 J. No. 4740 AA-PA Konstantinopel 170 telegram 70.

34. Rössler to Embassy, Aleppo, August 16, 1915 J. No. 4745 AA-PA Konstantinopel 170 telegram 71; Rössler to Embassy, Aleppo, August 24,

1915 J. No. 4917 Ibid. telegram 77; Rössler to Embassy, Aleppo, August 31, 1915 J. No. 5045 Ibid. telegram 87; Hohenlohe to Rössler, Pera, September 5, 1915 J. No. 1962 AA-PA Konsulat Aleppo, Pkt. 1-2 telegram 63.

35. The author refers here to the gendarmes that accompanied the deportation caravans.

36. Vahram Daderian, *Our Story*, Manuscript, Eskijian Family Archives, Altadena, CA.

37. Ibid.

38. Hagobian-Taft, Rebirth, p.56-57.

39. Memoirs of Naomie Ouzounian, enclosure to Naomie Ouzounian to Luther Eskijian, Palatine, Ill, April 24, 1982 Eskijian Family Archives, Altadena, CA.

40. Shukru Aghazarian, "Odyssey of an Armenian youth who learned he could tackle the Turk with bribery" in Paren Kazanjian (ed.), *The Cilician Armenian Ordeal*, Boston, MA: Hye Intentions Inc., 1989 p.4.

41. Elmasd Santoorian, "A nurse's odyssey: from Marash to Aleppo and back" in Kazanjian, *Cilician Armenian Ordeal*, p.445.

42. Nazareth Yacoobian, "From the 1895-96 Frying Pan to the 1915-1922 Fires" in Kazanjian, *Cilician Armenian Ordeal*, p.487.

43. Khoren K. Davidson, *Odysee of an Armenian of Zeitoun*. With a Foreword by Aram Saroyan, New York: Vantage Press, 1985 p.82. In fact, Goltz was deeply impressed by the sight of Katma. On arrival at Aleppo he wrote to wife about his impressions. Goltz to Ms. Goltz, Aleppo, November 22, 1915, in Colmar Von der Goltz, *Denkwürdigkeiten*, ed. by. Friedrich Von der Goltz and Wolfgang Foerster, Berlin: Mittler & Sohn, 1929 p. 428.

44. Rössler to Bethmann Hollweg, Aleppo, September 3, 1915 A 28019 AA-PA Türkei 183/38 No. 1950; Rössler to Embassy, Aleppo, September 12, 1915 J. No. 5308 AA-PA Konstantinopel 170 telegram 99; Rössler to Embassy, Aleppo, September 24, 1915 J. No. 5788 AA-PA Konstantinopel 97 telegram 104. See also: Jackson to Morgenthau, Aleppo, August 19, 1915 US-NA Record Group 59. 867.4016/148 No. 346; Jackson to Morgenthau, Aleppo, September 29, 1915 US-NA Record Group 59. 867.4016/219 No. 3823 in, Sarafian (compiler), *United States Official Documents*, vol. 1, pp.53-54, 94-104. In this report, Jackson

provided detailed statistical material on the extent of railway deportation and the number of victims.

45. Rössler to Embassy, Aleppo, September 9, 1915 J. No. 5240 AA-PA Konstantinopel 170 telegram 93; Rössler to Embassy, Aleppo, September 14, 1915 J. No. 5343 Ibid. telegram 100; Rössler to Embassy, Aleppo, September 18, 1915 J. No. 5421 Ibid. telegram 101. German military physicians described the epidemics and the mortality in detail. See: Viktor Schilling, *Kriegshygienische Erfahrungen in der Türkei (Cilicien, Nordsyrien)*, Leipzig: J. A. Barth, (Beihefte zum Archiv für Schiffs- und Tropenhygiene, Bd. 25) 1921.

46. Rössler to Hohenlohe, Aleppo, September 27, 1915 J. No. 5779 AA-PA Konstantinopel 170 No. 2130.

47. Ibid.

48. Niepage, Aleppo, October 15, 1915 enclosure in Neurath to Bethmann Hollweg, Pera, October 30, 1915 A 32368 AA-PA Türkei 183/ 39 No. 855; Hoffmann to Embassy, Aleppo, October 19, 1915 J. No. 9279 AA-PA Konstantinopel 97 No. 2385. The quote originates from an English translation of Niepage's account that was published in Britain. Johannes Lepsius had edited it. Martin Niepage, *The Horror's of Aleppo Seen by a German Eye-Witness*, London: T. Fisher Unwin, 1917 p.6, 9, 12. Niepage notes that Vice-consul Hoffmann took several photos in the han. He sent three of these to Berlin, which are reproduced here. Lepsius had added the reference on cut-off childrens' hands to the text. While the original manuscript does not contain this detail, another source confirms its veracity. A German navy officer had visited the destroyed village of Tell Ermen near Mardin. The Ottoman authorities had massacred the population. Near the burned down church he saw fragments of children's hands and women's hair. Engelking to Comand of the Fleet, Constantinople, November 11, 1915 G.B. N. 8289 Bundesarchiv, Abteilungen Freiburg, Reichsmarine 40/434. The massacres of Armenians and other Christian minorities in the area of Mardin and at Tell Ermen have been described in: Hyacinthe Simon, *Mardine. La ville heroïque. Autel et tombeau de l'Arménie (Asie Mineure) durant les massacres de 1915*, edited by Naji Naaman, introduction by Georges Yeghiayan, Jounieh: Maison Naaman pour la culture, 1991; Marco Impagliazzo, *Una finestra sul massacro. Documenti inediti sulla strage degli armeni (1915-1916)*, Milano: Guerini e Associati, 2000.

49. Hoffmann to Embassy, Aleppo, October 18, 1915 J. No. 5989 AA-PA Konstantinopel 171 telegram 123; Hoffmann to Embasy, Aleppo, October 18, 1915 J. No. 5990 Ibid. telegram 124; Hoffmann to Embassy, Aleppo, October 18, 1915 J. No. 2298 AA-PA Konsulat Aleppo, Pkt. 2

Bd.3 telegram 126; Hoffmann to Embassy, Aleppo, October 19, 1915 J. No. 2296 Ibid. telegram 125; Hoffmann to Embassy, Aleppo, October 21, 1915 J. No. 6046 AA-PA Konstantinopel 171 telegram 129; Rössler to Embassy, Aleppo, November 5, 1915 J. No. 9462 AA-PA Konstantinopel 409 telegram 157; Hoffmann to Embassy, Alexandretta, November 8, 1915 J. No. 284 AA-PA Konstantinopel 172 No. 944.

50. Rössler to Embassy, Aleppo, October 27, 1915 J. No. 6211 AA-PA Konstantinopel 171 telegram 140.

51. Rössler to Embassy, Aleppo, November 6, 1915 J. No. 2476 AA-PA Konsulat Aleppo, Pkt. 3 Bd. 3 telegram 155. Erden, *Suriye Hâtýralarý*, p.123.

52. Rössler to Bethmann Hollweg, Aleppo, November 8, 1915 A 35045 AA-PA Türkei 183/40 No. 2511.

53. Hoffmann to Embassy, Alexandrette, November 8, 1915 J. No. 284 AA-PA Konstantinopel 172 No. 944; Rössler to Embassy, Aleppo, November 15, 1915 J. No. 9986 AA-PA Konstantinopel 409 telegram 166; Anonymous, "The Migration of the Armenians to Der Zor," Aleppo, November 11, 1915 enclosure to Rössler to Bethmann Hollweg, Aleppo, November 16, 1915 A 35047 AA-PA Türkei 183/40 No. 2078.

54. Rössler to Bethmann Hollweg, Aleppo, December 20, 1915 A 468 AA-PA Türkei 183/40 No. 2881. On the origins of denial see: Kaiser, *Le génocide arménien*; idem, "Dall'impero alla repubblica: le continuità del negazionismo turco" (Forthcoming Milano: Bruno Mondadori,2001).

55. Rössler to Bethmann Hollweg, Aleppo, November 30, 1915 A 36213 AA-PA Türkei 183/40 No. 2725; Rohner, Aleppo, n.d., enclosure to Rössler to Metternich, Aleppo, February 19, 1916 J. No. 2317 Aa-PA Konstantinopel 99 No. 392.

56. Bryce/Toynbee, *Treatment*; Riggs, *Days of Tragedy*; Ara Sarafian, "The Paper Trail: the American State Department and the Report of Committee on Armenian Atrocities," *Revue du monde arménien moderne et contemporain*, 1 (1994), pp.127-160. James L. Barton (compiler), *"Turkish Atrocities." Statements of American Missionaries on the Destruction of Christian Communities in Ottoman Turkey, 1915-1917*, Ann Arbor, MI: Gomidas Institute, 1998. Some of the missionaries kept diaries which were smuggled out of the country after they had left. Bertha B. Morley, *Marsovan 1915: The Diaries of Bertha Morley*, (ed. by Hilmar Kaiser), 2nd edition, Ann Arbor, MI: Gomidas Institute, 2000; Tacy Atkinson, *"The German, the Turk and the*

Devil Made a Triple Alliance." Harpoot Diaries, 1908-1917, (With a fore-word by J. Michael Hagopian), Princeton, NJ: Gomidas Institute, 2000.

57. On the political activities of the ABCFM see: Robert L. Daniel, *American Philanthropy in the Near East, 1820-1960*, Athens, Ohio: Ohio University Press, 1970; Joseph L. Grabill, *Protestant Diplomacy and the Near East. Missionary Influence on American Policy, 1810-1927*, Minneapolis: University of Minnesota Press, 1971.

58. On Peet, see Louise Jenison Peet, *No Less Honor: The Biography of William Wheelock Peet*, n.p.: Privately Printed, 1939.

59. See for instance: George E. White, *Adventuring with Anatolia College*, Grinnell, Iowa: Herald-Register Publishing Company, 1940.

60. Barton, *Near East Relief.*

61. Sarafian (compiler), *United States Official Documents*, Vols. 1-3.

62. Uwe Feigel, *Das evangelische Deutschland und Armenien. Die Armenierhilfe deutscher evangelischer Christen seit dem Ende des 19. Jahrhunderts im Kontext der deutsch-türkischen Beziehungen*, Göttingen: Vandenhoeck & Ruprecht, (Kirche und Konfession, Band 28) 1989; Norbert Saupp, *Das Deutsche Reich und die Armenische Frage 1878-1914*, PhD dissertation, University of Köln, 1990.

63. Christoph Dinkel, "Die schweizerische Armenierhilfe. Chronik von 1896 bis in die Zwischenkriegszeit" in Hans-Lukas Kieser (ed.), *Die armenische Frage und die Schweiz (1896-1923)*, Zürich: Chronos Verlag, 1999 pp. 187-210.

64. "The suggested public condemnation of an ally during the present war would be a measure unlike any in history. Our sole object is to keep Turkey on our side until the end of the war, no matter if Armenians perish over that or not. In the face of a longer continuing war we will still neet the Turks very much" Kaiser, *Le génocide arménien*, p.82.

65. Feigel, *Das evangelische Deutschland*, pp.230-236.

66. Hans-Lukas Kieser, *Der verpasste Friede. Mission, Ethnie and Staat in den Ostprovinzen der Türkei 1839-1938*, Zürich: Chronos, 2000 p.355.

67. Schuchardt to AA, Frankfurt/M., June 9, 1915 A 18714 AA-PA Türkei 183/37; Neurath to Schuchardt, Pera, June 29, 1915 A 20791 Ibid. No.3898; Schuchardt to AA, Frankfurt/M., July 6, 1915 A 20929 Ibid.; AA to Schuchardt, Berlin, July 14, 1915 zu A 20928/21158

Ibid.; Schuchardt to AA, Frankfurt/M, July 16, 1915 A 21763 Ibid; Schuchardt to AA, Frankfurt/M, July 17, 1915 A 21765 Ibid.

68. Schuchardt to AA, Frankfurt/M, August 20, 1915 A 24658 AA-PA Türkei 183/38; Schuchardt to Bethmann Hollweg, Frankfurt/M, August 21, 1915 A 24748 Ibid.; Schuchardt to AA, Frankfurt/M, August 21, 1915 A 24724 Ibid.

69. Zimmermann to Hohenlohe, Berlin, August 25, 1915 zu A 24658 AA-PA Türkei 183/38 telegram 1589; Hohenlohe to AA, Pera, August 27, 1915 A 25227 Ibid. telegram 1914; Schuchardt to AA, Frankfurt/M, September 2, 1915 A 25988 Ibid.; Schuchardt to Göppert, Frankfurt/M., September 20, 1915 A 31138 Ibid.; Schuchardt to AA, Frankfurt/M., October 11, 1915 A 29546 AA-PA Türkei 183/39.

70. Schuchardt to Bethmann Hollweg, Frankfurt/M., October 4, 1915 A 28952 AA-PA Türkei 183/39; Schuchardt to AA, Frankfurt/M., October 11, 1915 A 29546 Ibid.; Zimmermann to Wangenheim, Berlin, October 15, 1915 zu A 29546 Ibid.; Zimmermann to Schuchardt, Berlin, October 15, 1915 Ibid.; Schuchardt to Rosenberg, Frankfurt/M., October 23, 1915 A 30773 Ibid.; Neurath to AA, Pera, October 24, 1915 A 30744 Ibid. telegram 2547; Rosenberg to Schuchardt, Berlin, October 25, 1915 zu A 30744 Ibid. telegram; Schuchardt to AA, Frankfurt/M., October 26, 1915 A 31038 Ibid.; Zimmermann to Embassy, Berlin, October 26, 1915 J. No. 6127 AA-PA Konstantinopel 171 telegram 2048; Neurath to AA, Pera, October 26, 1915 A 31002 AA-PA Türkei 183/39 telegram 2474; Rosenberg to Schuchardt, Berlin, October 27, 1915 zu A 31002 Ibid. telegram; Schuchardt to AA, Frankfurt/M., October 28, 1915 A 31189 Ibid. telegram.

71. Oberndorff to Bethmann Hollweg, Christiania, October 29, 1915 A 31605 AA-PA Türkei 183/39 No.479; Romberg to Bethmann Hollweg, Berne, October 24, 1915 A 31258 Ibid. No. 931; Axenfeld to Bethmann Hollweg, Berlin, October 18, 1915 A 30410 Ibid.; Erzberger to Bethmann Hollweg, Berlin, October 30, 1915 A 31375 Ibid.; Bethmann Hollweg to Schreiber, Berlin, November 12, 1915 A 33275 Ibid.; Bethmann Hollweg to Erzberger, Berlin, November 12, 1915 A 33276 Ibid.; Zimmermann to Schreiber, Berlin, November 18, 1915 A 33208 Ibid. For a discussion of the Swiss efforts on behalf of the Ottoman Armenians see the contributions in: Kieser (ed.), *Die armenische Frage*. On the impact of international public opinion on German policies see: Kaiser, *Le genocide arménien*.

72. Zimmermann to Neurath, Berlin, November 9, 1915 A 32383 AA-PA
     Türkei 183/39 No. 848.

73. Schuchardt to Rosenberg, Constantinople, November 12, 1915 J. No.
     – AA-PA Konstantinopel 171; Schuchardt to Rosenberg, Constantino-
     ple, November 22, 1915 A 33915 AA-PA Türkei 183/140; Schuchardt
     to AA, Constantinople, December 3, 1915 A 35310 Ibid; Metternich to
     Bethmann Hollweg, Pera, November 23, 1915 A 34772 Ibid. No.692.
     Library of Congress, Morgenthau Diaries, Entries November 12, 17,
     18, 1915.

74. Rössler to Embassy, Aleppo, August 31, 1915 J. No. 1923 AA-PA Kon-
     sulat Aleppo, Pkt. 1 Bd. 1-2 telegram 88; Rössler to Embassy, Aleppo,
     September 7, 1915 J. No. 1962 Ibid. telegram 90; Rössler to Embassy,
     Aleppo, September 10, 1915 J. No. 2005 Ibid. telegram 94; Rosenberg,
     Berlin, November 1, 1915 marginal note to Rosenberg to Schuchardt,
     Berlin, October 27, 1915 zu A 31002 AA-PA Türkei 183/39 telegram;
     Minister to Marash District, Constantinople, September 22, 1915
     EUM Special No. 37 BOA.DH.ÞFR 56/121.

75. Shepard to Peet, Aleppo, November 5, 1915 ABCFM-NY, Relief
     1915-1916. Shepard Riggs, *Shepard*, p.191.

76. Schäfer, born in 1879 in Schwelm, lost her parents at a young age and
     grew up with her grandmother. After being trained in a hospital in
     Wuppertal, she joined the "Hülfsbund" in 1901 and worked in Marash.
     Deutscher Hilfsbund, Bad Homburg, Personnel Biographies.

77. Rohner, born in 1876 in Basel, studied education, modern languages,
     and mathematics. She joined the "Hülfsbund" in 1898 and went to Con-
     stantinople in 1899 and moved on to Marash in 1901. She worked in the
     German orphanage and supervised Bible women work in the region.
     Gedenkschrift für Beatrice Rohner, Wüstenrot: Kurt Reith Verlag, 1947.

78. Biography of Hovhannes Eskijian by Gulenia H. Eskijian. Manuscript.
     Eskijian Family Archives, Altadena, CA.

79. Anonymous, A Page About Rev. H. Eskijian's Life, n.p., n.d., Eskijian
     Family Archives, Altadena, CA.

80. Haleblian became one of the few survivors of the underground net-
     work. 44 years later he re-established contact with the family of the
     Reverend. Hagop Haleblian to Luther Eskijian, Beirut, January 1960,
     Eskijian Family Archives.

81.   Memoirs of Garabed Keverian in *Tchanasser* (1951 No.24) as quoted in Shnorhokian p.22. See also: Minassian: *Many Hills Yet to Climb. Memoirs of an Armenian Deportee*, Santa Barbara, CA: Jim Cook Publ., 1986., p.101.

82.   Kirkor Ankout, Le Kasildikh d'Alepp, in Kévorkian, Témoignages, pp.102-104. Shnorhokian, however, identifies 'karlik' as the location of the camp. "Karlik was a hill of rocks and cliffs and crevices outside Aleppo, one hour's walk from the city. Hundreds and thousands of Armenian refugees coming from all over Turkey [sic] would be stationed there for days or weeks to be driven to their final death in the burning deserts of Syria and Iraq." M. H. Shnorhokian, A Pioneer During the Armenian Genocide. Rev. Hovhannes Eskijian, n.p., 1989, Manuscript, p.15 Eskijian Family Archives, Altadena, CA. Evidently, more than one transit camps for deportees existed on the outskirts of Aleppo.

83.   Memoirs of Naomie Ouzounian, enclosure to Naomie Ouzounian to Luther Eskijian, Palatine, Ill, April 24, 1982 Eskijian Family Archives, Altadena, CA.

84.   Statement by Sarkis F. Consulian, n.p., n.d., Eskijian Family Archives, Altadena, CA. Noomen (Pseudonym), Reverend Hovhannes Eskijian in Aleppo, in, *Gotchnag* 33,6 (February 10, 1923) (translated by George B. Kooshian).

85.   Eflatoon E. Elmajian, *Reverend Hovhannes Eskijian. How I Know Him*, Manuscript, n.d., Eskijian Family Archives, Altadena, CA. Elmajian's experiences were by no means exceptional. His landlord's actions followed an established pattern. James Sutherland described the situation of Armenian tenants as follows: "…the Turkish police department in the city started to raid the houses and arrest the Armenian deportees. They would send them to the concentration camps and then deport them to Deir-el-zor for slaughter. The Syrian natives of Aleppo would rent their rooms for cash at a very exorbitant price, receiving the money in advance, and the next day they would go to the Turkish police station reporting the presence of Armenians in their house. The Armenians would be raided and the whole family would be deported for slaughter and the owner of the house would look for a new tenant and a new victim. This practice was repeated many, many times. Unless the Armenian deportees had some gold money to bribe the policemen with, their goose was cooked. One can imagine the precarious

position the helpless people were in, including ourselves." James K. Sutherland, *Adventures of an Armenian Boy. Reminiscences of Dr. James K. Sutherland*, Ann Arbor, MI: The Ann Arbor Press, 1964 p.122.

86.   Minassian, *Many Hills* p.92.

87.   At times, Arshavir communicated his findings directly to the central government at Constantinople. He was evidently a top agent. Ministry of the Interior to Aleppo Province, Constantinople, August 21, 1918 Kalemi Mahsûs 4566 BOA.DH.ÞFR, nr 90/188 Eflatoon E. Elmajian, 1982 p. 52. Idem, *Reverend Hovhannes Eskijian.* "Upon my return to work at the Pharmacy, my colleague Mihran Najarian warned me that a malicious member of the Turkish secret police, Arshavir, was in town and that he had come to the Pharmacy to buy aspirin tablets. 'Do not speak Armenian while Arshavir is in the store!' Mihran warned me again and again. 'Also, do not show excitement or any special interest in him, whe he comes back.' We walked in constant fear in those days, but we also worked with feverish hope to save those we could save." Vahram K. Goekjian, *Voyage Through Stormy Seas. Part I: The Years of Peril and Bereavement*, New York, N.Y.: n.p., 1983 p.52. Davidson confirms the importance of the agent and reports on his end: "I asked the druggist if he knew the man. He told me the man was a spy and his name was Arshavir Yasian. "I do not know how you can get rid of him and save your neck," the druggist told me. The druggist also stated that the spy had been instrumental in the hanging of several revolutionary Hunchakians in Constantinople. From there he had been sent to Aleppo to hunt and find deserters and disguised persons and deliver them to the authorities. "Let me tell you that this man had a quarrel with the governor," he said. "He sent a telegram to Talaat threatening that if the governor remained in Aleppo, he would leave. Soon after, the governor was removed." p.150 "Arshavir, disguised as a French soldier, arrived in Adana on his way to Konya. However, pursuit of him continued. In Adana he was invited to a family party. There he met many acquaintances who knew of his disguise. After eating and drinking, one of the friends made a toast. "Brethren," he began, "the agonizing days of the Armenians are over. The Armenian has risen again. The revengeful and cruel Turk could not annihilate him. Come, let us have a cleaning account. There were many among us too mean, vile Armenians, who caused the death of many of our innocent people." He then faced Arshavir and said, "You, the betrayer of your fellowmen, you do not de-

serve to live anymore. Boys, bring the electric wire and wrap it around his neck." The next day, his body was found in a six-foot-deep ditch. This was the end of the one who had even caused the recall of the governor of Aleppo, by his telegramm to Talaat Pasha in Constantinople." Davidson, *Odysee*, p.221.

88. "For him all young men and young girls were Protestants, with his permit in his hand he used to take them out of the train." Elmajian, Rev. Hovhannes Eskijian.

89. Elfatoon E. Elmajian, Testimony, n.p., n.d., Eskijian Family Archives, Altadena, CA.

90. Minassian, *Many Hills*, p. 89, 95. Juskalian contracted typhus while helping deportess and died in March 1916.

91. Garabed Keverian to Luther Eskijian, Beirut, August 12, 1958 Eskijian Family Archives, Altadena, CA.

92. Minassian, *Many Hills*, pp.94-95, 102.

93. Ibid. p.93 see also: Ibid. p.97.

94. Memorandum by Walter M. Geddes, November 8, 1915, in, Toynbee/ Bryce, Treatment, p.559-560.

95. Minassian, *Many Hills*, p.86.

96. Elfatoon E. Elmajian, Testimony, n.p., n.d., Eskijian Family Archives, Altadena, CA. In another manuscript, Elmajian gives additonal details about how Rev. Eskijian found the children: "…[he] told us that story of the child sucking his dead mother's breast." Elmajian, Rev. *Hovhannes Eskijian.*

97. Memoirs of Naomie Ouzounian, enclosure to Naomie Ouzounian to Luther Eskijian, Palatine, Ill, April 24, 1982 Eskijian Family Archives, Pasadena, CA.

98. Minassian, *Many Hills*, p.105.

99. Ibid.

100. Sisag Solakian to Gulenia Eskijian, Kilis, March 29, 1916 Eskijian Family Archives, Altadena, CA; Loutfi Sayegh to Gulenia Eskijian, Der Zor, April 1, 1916 Ibid.; H. V. Najarian to Gulenia Eskijian, Sebka, April 2, 1916 Ibid., Mariam Koundakjian to Gulenia Eskijian, Entilli, April 3, 1916 Ibid.

101. Minassian, Many Hills, p. 88, 97.

102. "Mrs. Eskijian took many of the teenage girls with her, because the police investigators would take them away for their leaders or would pick one for themselves." Ibid. p.105.

103. 103 Ibid. p.110.

104. 104 Ibid. p.120.

105. 105 "Miss Rohner tried to see the authorities, even the governor of the state, to plead for our protection and safety. She told him that she needed us for the education of the little children. Soon we were called to her officer one by one. She told us that she had failed. The governor turned her down because he said that he had orders from party head-quarers of Ethehad, directly from Tallet Pasha. Miss Rohner told me to leave the city before it was too late, for it was too dangerous to stay at my age." Ibid. pp.122-123.

106. 106 Ibid. p.104.

107. Memoirs of Garabed Keverian in Tchanasser (1951 No.24) as quoted in Shnorhokian p.22. On the Dersim Kurds see: Riggs, *Days of Tragedy*, pp.108-117.

108. Schäfer, n.p., November 16, 1915, Rohner, [Marash], November 16, 1915, Schäfer, n.p., December 1, 1915, enclosures to Schuchardt to AA, Frankfurt/M., January 26, 1916 A 2682 AA-PA Türkei 183/40. Johann Heinrich Mordtmann, the head of the Armenian desk at the German embassy, received the reports and permitted their forwarding to Peet and Schuchardt. Mordtmann, Pera, December 27, 1915 J. No. 11710 AA-PA Konstantinopel 98. The reports were later published in Toynbee/Bryce, *Treatment*, pp.469-472; Rohner, Aleppo, April 1916, enclosure to Metternich to Bethmann Hollweg, April 28, 1916 A 11471 AA-PA Türkei 183/42 No. 201.

109. Rohner, Aleppo, December 29, 1915 copy, enclosure to Schuchardt to AA, Frankfurt/M., February 14, 1916 A 4240 AA-PA Türkei 183/41.

110. Kress von Kressenstein, *Mit den Türken*, pp.135-136. Busse, Aleppo, December 1915/January 1916, Bundesarchiv, Abteilungen Freiburg, Reichsmarine 40/504, War Diaries Commander Busse, December 16, 1915 – February 22, 1916 folio 56-57. The Kochs were very influential at Aleppo. Martha Koch spoke fluently Arabic and entertained best relations with German officers passing through the city. Her house was the social cen-

ter of German society in Aleppo. Her paramount role is also attested to by the fact she was a close friend of German General Colmar Von der Goltz, the commander of the Ottoman troops in Iraq in early 1916. Koch was also a collector of antiquities and an advisor on acquisitions for German museums. The relations between the Kochs and consul Rössler were, however, bad and both families did not exchange visits for a long time. Thus, it is not surprising that the German consul was not present at the breakfast meeting. Wilhelm His, *Die Front der Ärzte*, Bielefeld: Velhagen und Klasing, 1931 pp.153-154, 220-221. Gerold Von Gleich, *Vom Balkan nach Bagdad. Militärisch-politische Erinnerungen an den Orient*, Berlin: Otto Scherl, 1921 pp.91-92. Aram Andonian, who survived in Aleppo in the underground, attested to Ms. Koch's work on behalf of the Armenians in Aleppo as well: Andonian, *Documents officiels*, pp.58-59.

111. Rohner to Mordtmann, Marash, December 15, 1915 J. No. 120 AA-PA Konstantinopel 98; Rohner, Aleppo, December 29, 1915 copy, enclosure to Schuchardt to AA, Frankfurt/M., February 14, 1916 A 4240 AA-PA Türkei 183/41. Schuchardt to AA, Frankfurt/M., December 23, 1915 IIId 14 AA-PA Geistliche Sachen Nr. 120 a adh. Deutscher Hülfsbund für christliches Liebeswerk im Orient Bd. 1. copy

112. Rohner to Peet, Aleppo, January 2, 1916 ABCFM-NY, Relief 1915-1916.

113. Jackson to Peet, Aleppo, December 30, 1915 ABCFM-NY, Relief 1915-16. An intercepted U.S. consular report has been recently published by the Turkish authorities. Davis to Morgenthau, Harpoot, August 23, 1915, in, Türkiye Cumhuriyeti, Baþbakanlýk Devlet Arþivleri Genel Müdürlüðü, Osmanlý Arþivi Daire Bakanlýðý, *Osmanlý Belgelerinde Ermeniler (1915-1920)*, Ankara: Baþbakanlýk Basýmevi, 1994, pp.88-89.

114. Schäfer to Peet, Harunje, January 2, 1916 ABCFM-NY, Relief 1915-1916; Rohner to Peet, Aleppo, January 2, 1916 Ibid. The women conducted their correspondence in German. Thus, the letters had to be translated for Peet into English.

115. Mordtmann, Pera, January 10, 1916 marginal note to Rössler to Embassy, Aleppo, January 2, 1916 J. No. 63 AA-PA Konstantinopel 98 telegram 1; Mordtmann to Peet, Pera, January 26, 1916 J. No. auf 741 Ibid.; Metternich to Rössler, Pera, January 6, 1916 J. No. ad 63 Ibid. telegram 7; Rössler to Embassy, Aleppo, January 11, 1916 J. No. 405 Ibid. telegram 7; Metternich to Rössler, Pera, January 20, 1916 J. No. zu 405 Ibid. telegram 16; Jackson to Embassy, Aleppo, January, 20, 1916 ABCFM-NY, Relief 1915-1916; Peet to Morgenthau, Constanti-

nople, January 22, 1916 Ibid.; Rössler to Metternich, Aleppo, January 29, 1916 No. 257 copy enclosure to Metternich to Bethmann Hollweg, Pera, February 17, 1916 A 4895 AA-PA Türkei 183/41 No.1490; Metternich to Bethmann Hollweg, Pera, April 4, 1916 A 9024 AA-PA Türkei 183/42 No. 3749.

116. Metternich to Rössler, Pera, January 17, 1916 J. No. zu 573 AA-PA Konstantinopel 98 telegram 13. On the concentration camp at Bab see Kévorkian, *Le sort*, pp.23-24 and Idem, *Témoignages*, 75-92.

117. Jackson to Peet, Aleppo January 20, 1916 ABCFM-NY, Relief 1915-916.

118. Shiragian to Rössler, Aleppo, January 10, 1916 J. No. 71 AA-PA Konsulat Aleppo, Pkt. 2 Bd.3. Reverend Aharon Shiragian worked closely with Rohner since he knew her from Marash. He had been deported from Marash on May 17, 1915; Beatrice Rohner, Report on Relief Work in Aleppo January 1 – June 1, enclosure to Rössler to Bethmann Hollweg, June 17, 1916 A 17939 AA-PA Türkei 183 No. 1703; Abraham H. Hartunian, *Neither To Laugh Nor To Weep*, transl. by Vartan Hartunian, 2nd ed. Intro. by Marjorie Housepian Dobkin, Boston, MA: NAASR, 1986 p.57.

119. Rössler to Metternich, Aleppo, January 29, 1916 No. 257 copy enclosure to Metternich to Bethmann Hollweg, Pera, February 17, 1916 A 4895 AA-PA Türkei 183/41 No.1490.

120. Rössler to Embassy, Aleppo, January 10, 1916 J. No. – AA-PA Konstantinopel 172 telegram 5; Rössler to Metternich, Aleppo, J. No. 7260 Ibid. No.236; Rössler to Metternich, Aleppo, January 28, 1916 J. No. 539 Ibid. No.247; Rössler to Metternich, Aleppo, February 9, 1916 J. No. 526 Ibid. telegram 21; Rössler to Bethmann Hollweg, Aleppo, February 9, 1916 A 5498 AA-PA Türkei 183/41 No. 366; Rohner, "Report on Relief Work in Aleppo January 1 – June 1, 1916," Aleppo, June 1916 enclosure to Rössler to Bethmann Hollweg, Aleppo, June 17, 1916 A 17939 AA-PA Türkei 183/43 No. 1703.

121. Rössler to AA, Aleppo, February 22, 1916 A 5064 AA-PA Türkei 183/41 telegram 3; Rössler to Embassy, Aleppo, February 23, 1916 J. No. 2166 AA-PA Konstantinopel 99 telegram 30; Rössler to Embassy, Aleppo, February 29, 1916 J. No. 763 AA-PA Konstantinopel 172 telegram 33.

122. Zimmermann to Romberg, Berlin, February 26, 1916 A 6654 AA-PA

Türkei 183/41 No.120; Zimmermann to Embassy, Berlin, March 5, 1916 A 6512 Ibid. telegram 313; Zimmermann to Romberg, Berlin March 17, 1916 A zu 6654 Ibid. No. 189; Metternich to Rössler, Pera, March 7, 1916 J. No. ad 261 AA-PA Konstantinopel 99 telegram 41; Rössler to Embassy, Aleppo, March 9, 1916 J. No. 2750 Ibid. telegram 41; Metternich to Bethmann Hollweg, Pera, March 10, 1916 A 6512 AA-PA Türkei 183/41 No. 390; Metternich to Bethmann Hollweg, Pera, March 27, 1916 IIId 1672 AA-PA Geistliche Sachen Nr. 120 a adh. Deutscher Hülfsbund für christliches Liebeswerk im Orient Bd. 1 telegram 472; Zimmermann to Romberg, Berlin, May 5, 1916 zu A 11471 AA-PA Türkei 183/42 No. 267.

123. Rössler to Embassy, Aleppo, March 1, 1916 J. No. 2456 AA-PA Konstantinopel 99 telegram 34; Rössler to Embassy, Aleppo, March 6, 1916 J. No. 2659 Ibid. telegram 35; Rössler to Embassy, Aleppo, March 10, 1916 J. No. 2838 Ibid. telegram 37; Metternich to Rössler, Pera, March 16, 1916 J. No. ad 3028 Ibid. telegram 44; Rössler to Embassy, Aleppo, March 27, 1916 J. No. 3464 AA-PA Konstantinopel 100 telegram 46; Rössler to Embassy, Aleppo, April 1, 1916 J. No. 3702 Ibid. telegram 51.

124. Ali Seydi to Ministry of the Interior, Constantinople, January 21, 1916. The document is published in *Documents sur les Arméniens-Ottoman*, vol. 2, [Ankara]: Présidence du conseil, Direction générale de la presse et de l'information, n.d. pp.106-107 No.1923 (119). The book is a translation of the journal Askeri Tarih Belgeleri Dergisi 83 (1983). Talaat to Adrianopel, Adana, Angora, Bitlis, Aleppo, Broussa, Diarbekir, Syria, Sivas, Trebizond, Konia, Kharpert provinces, Ourfa, Izmit, Afion, Mersina, Nigde, Djanik, Zor, Karesi, Kutahia, Eskishehir, Marash districts, Constantinople, January 30, 1916 EUM BOA.DH.ÞFR 60/183. The document has been published by Þinasi Orel and Süreyya Yuca, *The Talât Pasha Telegrams. Historical Fact or Armenian Fiction?* Nicosia: K. Rustem & Brother, 1986 p.238.

125. Ministry to Kharpert, Aleppo provinces, Cesarea district, Constantinople, February 9, 1916 EUM 2nd Department BOA.DH.ÞFR 60/281.

126. Talaat to Aleppo, Adana, Mossoul, Diarbekir provinces, Ourfa, Zor districts, Constantinople, February 13, 1916 EUM Spec. 6806 BOA. DH.ÞFR 61/32.

127. Talaat to Adrianopel, Adana, Angora, Bitlis, Aleppo, Broussa, Diar-

bekir, Syria, Sivas, Trebizond, Kastamonou, Konia, Kharpert, Mossoul provinces Ourfa, Izmidt, Bolu, Canik, Zor, Karesi, Cesarea, Mersin, Kutahia Eskishehir, Marash, Afion, Nigde districts, Constantinople, March 23, 1916 EUM General 44298 BOA.DH.ÞFR 62/90.

128. Talaat to Adrianopel, Adana, Angora, Bitlis, Aleppo, Broussa, Diarbekir, Syria, Sivas, Trebizond, Kastamonou, Konya, Mamuretülaziz, Mossoul provinces, Ourfa, Ismidt, Afion, Marash, Nigde, Bolou, Canik, Zor, Karesi, Cesarea, Mersin, Kutahia, Eskishehir districts, Constantinople, April 3, 1916 EUM Special 71 BOA.DH.ÞFR 62/210.

129. Metternich to Rössler, Pera, March 28, 1916 J. No. 1056 AA-PA Konstantinopel 172 telegram 52; Metternich to Bethmann Hollweg, Pera, March 29, 1916 A 8702 AA-PA Türkei 183/42 No. 139; Metternich to Bethmann Hollweg, Pera, April 28, 1916 A 11470 Ibid. No. 200.

130. Rössler to Embassy, Aleppo, March 23, 1916 J. No. 1021 AA-PA Konstantinopel 172 telegram 41; Rössler to Embassy, Aleppo March 23, 1916 J. No. 1022 Ibid. telegram 42; Metternich to Bethmann Hollweg, Pera, March 27, 1916 A 8373 AA-PA Türkei 183/41 No. 131; Rössler to Embassy, Aleppo, April 6, 1916 J. No. 1122 AA-PA Konstantinopel 172 telegram 55; Rössler to Bethmann Hollweg, Aleppo, April 27, 1916 A 12911 AA-PA Türkei 183/42No. 1189.

131. Rössler to Embassy, Aleppo, April 7, 1916 J. No. 4054 AA-PA Konstantinopel 100 telegram 60; Rössler to Embassy, Aleppo, April 7, 1916 J. No. 4055 Ibid. telegram 61; Rössler to Embassy, Aleppo, April 8, 1916 J. No. 3986 Ibid. telegram 62; Rössler to Embassy, Aleppo, April 10, 1916 J. No. 4074 Ibid. telegram 64; Rössler to Embassy, Aleppo, April 12, 1916 J. No. 4136 Ibid. telegram 67; Rohner, Aleppo, n.d., enclosure to Rössler to Metternich, Aleppo, April 12, 1916 J. No. 4385 Ibid. No. 1033; Rössler to Embassy, Aleppo, April 18, 1916 J. No. 4429 Ibid. telegram 73; Rössler to Embassy, Aleppo, April 19, 1916 J. No. 4455 Ibid. telegram 74; Metternich to Rössler, Pera, April 21, 1916 J. No. 4452 Ibid. telegram 67; Rössler to Embassy, Aleppo, April 22, 1916 J. No. 4537 Ibid. telegram 76; Rössler to Embassy, Aleppo, May 13, 1916 J. No. 5318 Ibid. telegram 89; Metternich to Rössler, Pera, May 19, 1916 J. No. II 5239 Ibid. telegram 77; Rohner to Peet, Aleppo, April 24, 1916 ABCFM-NY Relief 1915-1916.

132. Rohner, Aleppo, June 26, 1916 enclosure to Rössler to Metternich,

Aleppo, June 29, 1916 J. No. II 6126 AA-PA Konstantinopel 101 No. 1822.

133. I owe the concept of the "second phase"of the genocide to Raymond Kévorkian.

134. Kaiser, *The Baghdad Railway*, pp.67-112.

135. Metternich to Bethmann Hollweg, Pera, July 10, 1916 A 18548AA-PA Türkei 183/43 No. 368.

136. Rössler to Embassy, Aleppo, June 3, 1916 J. No. II 5522 AA-PA Konstantinopel 100 telegram 102; Rössler to Embassy, Aleppo, June 18, 1916 J. No. 5762 Ibid. telegram 109; Rössler to Embassy, Aleppo, June 5, 1916 J. No. 1694 AA-PA Konstantinopel 172 telegram 104; Rohner, Aleppo, June 1916, enclosure to Rössler to Bethmann Hollweg, Aleppo, June, 17, 1916 A 17939 AA-PA Türkei 183/43 No. 1703.

137. Rössler to Embassy, Aleppo, May 13, 1916 J. No. 1502 AA-PA Konstantinopel 172 tel. 87; Rössler to Embassy, Aleppo, June 27, 1916 J. No. 1882 Ibid. telegram 117. Rössler to Bethmann Hollweg, Aleppo, June 17, 1916 A 17939 AA-PA Türkei 183/43 No. 1703; Rössler to Embassy, Aleppo, June 27, 1916 J. No. 1810 AA-PA Konsulat Aleppo, Pkt 2 Bd.5 telegram 118; Rössler to Metternich, Aleppo, June 29, 1916 J. No. II 6126 AA-PA Konstantinopel 101 No. 1822. The German embassy's intervention on behalf of the orphans is confirmed by a telegram of the Ottoman Ministry of the Interior. The Directorate for Public Security inquired with the provincial authorities at Aleppo if concerns existed leaving up to 320 children under Rohner's care. Ministry to Aleppo province, Constantinople, May 6, 1916 EUM Special 49 BOA, DH.ÞFR 63/225.

138. Rössler to Embassy, Aleppo, July 7, 1916 J. No. II 6044 AA-PA Konstantinopel 101 telegram 124; Rohner to Rössler, Aleppo, July 5, 1916 copy enclosure to Rössler to Metternich, Aleppo, July 8, 1916 J. No. II 6267 Ibid. No. 1909; Rössler to Metternich, Aleppo, July 19, 1916 II 6440 Ibid. No. 1911; Metternich to Rössler, Pera, July 25, 1916 J. No. zu II 6336 Ibid. telegram 103.

139. Rössler to Bethmann Hollweg, Aleppo, July 29, 1916 A 21629 AA-PA Türkei 18344 No. 2135.

140. Djebedjian to Rohner, Deir Zor, n.d. enclosure to Rohner to Peet, Aleppo, September 2, 1916 ABCFM-NY Relief 1915-1916.

141. Rössler to Embassy, Aleppo, August 13, 1916 J. No. 2405 AA-PA Konstantinopel 173 telegram 152; Bernau, Aleppo, [September 10], 1916 enclosure to Rössler to Bethmann Hollweg, Aleppo, September 20, 1916 A 28162 AA-PA Türkei 183/45 No. 2669. Rössler to Radowitz, Aleppo, November 5, 1916 J. No. II 8702 AA-PA Konstantinopel 101 No. 3045 (3 enclosures).

142. Rohner, Aleppo, November 6, 1916 enclosure to Rössler to Embassy, Aleppo, November 11, 1916 J. No. II 8702 AA-PA Konstantinopel 101 No. 3045; Rössler to Embassy, Aleppo, December 22, 1916 J. No. II 9309 Ibid. telegram 205; Rössler to Bethmann Hollweg, Aleppo, September 15, 1916 A 26934 AA-PA Türkei 183/44 No. 2605; Radowitz to Bethmann Hollweg, Pera, October 4, 1916 A 27493 Ibid. No.II 7596; Rohner to Rippenbach, Aleppo, November 24, 1916 copy enclosure to Rössler to Bethmann Hollweg, Aleppo, November 25, 1916 A 34236 AA-PA Türkei 183/45 No. 3173.

143. Rössler to Bethmann Hollweg, Aleppo, February 14, 1917 A 8613 AA-PA Türkei 183/46 No.299; Rössler to Embassy, Aleppo, March 4, 1917 II 1175 AA-PA Konstantinopel 101 telegram 19; Rössler to Bethmann, Hollweg, Aleppo, March 16, 1916 A 11348 AA-PA Türkei 183/47 No. 466; Beatrice Rohner, *Die Stunde ist gekommen. Märtyrerbilder aus der Jetztzeit*, Frankfurt/M.: Verlag Orient, [1919]. Given the fact that Edib took only those orphans under her control that were anyhow cared for, Erden's praise of the work seems to be misplaced. His claim that no Armenians were sent on orders of the Fourth Ottoman Army into the desert is not supported by the historical record, Erden, *Suriye Hâtýralarý*, p.123. Survivors remember Halide Edib's role during the genocide with great bitterness, particularly as American missionary circles promoted the Turkish nationalist in the 1920s. "My younger brother had been taken to Lebanon and placed in a Turkish orphanage opened by the infamous and lecherous favorite of Kemal Ataturk, Halide Hanum Edib Adivar, who wrote a couple of pious, unctuous books all but venerated in Western "liberal intellectual" circles - and even some visionary Western clergymen who thought she was a great, humane woman. But these orphanages were not opened out of humanitarian reasons but were meant to turkify the Armenian children who had been orphaned precisely by this Halide Edib's monstrous Young Turks." Stepan Dardooni, "Seminarian, Deportee, and Legionnaire" in Kazanjian, *Cilician*

Armenian Ordeal, p.210

144. Rössler to Embassy, Aleppo, February 10, 1917 J. No. 240 AA-PA Konsulat Aleppo, Pkt 3 Bd. 7 telegram 9.

145. For an account of Morley's life and the some of the surviving orphans see: *Not by Bread Alone: The Life of Bertha B. Morley*, written for her foster family, n.p.: College Press, 1967.

Endnotes for pages 60-68

1. Letter of Mrs. Yvenigi Jebijian, March 15, 1953, Aleppo, Syria.

2. The statement of the policeman is taken from a letter of Mrs. Rahel Megerdichian, dated January 20, 1959. Mrs. Megerdichian states that she heard it from an eyewitness who was trustworthy.

3. Rev. Garabed Tilkian, *Evangelical Challenge to the Genocide During World War One, 1914-1918*, December 28, 1981, Encino, California.

4. Reported by his wife, Mrs. Gulenia Eskijian

5. From his biography by Mrs. Gulenia Eskijian.

6. Ibid.

7. Ibid.

8. Ibid.

9. Ibid.

10. *A Pioneer During the Genocide, Rev. Hovhannes Eskijian, Informal Biography,* compiled by M.H. Shnorhokian, 1989.

11. Garabed Keverian, *Chanacer*, (Beirut, Lebanon, Principal of Armenian Evangelical School.)

12. Testimony of Sarkis Consulian who stayed in Rev. Eskijian's orphanage.

13. Rev. E. Elmajian testimonial.

14. Garabed Keverian, *Tchanaser*, 1951, No. 24. Translated article.

15. From an article written by John Minassian on the 10th anniversary of Rev. Eskijian's death. Mr. Minassian's life was saved through the efforts of Rev. Eskijian.

16. Testimony of Rahel Megerdichian. Her husband Dr. Samuel Megerdichian of Kessab, was a classmate of Rev. Eskijian in Central Turkey College.

17. Testimonial by Rev. E. Elmajian about the work of Rev. and Mrs. Eskijian.

18. Minassian, Tenth Anniversary article.

19. Yevnigi Jebijian letter.

20. Article in *Gotchnag* by Rev. E. Elmajian.

21.   Minassian, tenth anniversary article.

22.   Author Unknown, On the Occasion of the 10th Anniversary of Rev. Eskijian's death.

23.   Eulogy by John Minassian.

24.   Letter from Mrs. Gulenia H. Eskijian to her sister, Nouritza Hanum Ekmekjian, Aleppo, April 20, 1916.

25.   "To the Unforgettable Memory of Rev. Hovhannes Eskijian." by John Minassian, 3/25/1916.

26.   *A Pioneer During the Genocide, Rev. Hovhannes Eskijian,* informal biography compiled by M.H. Shnorhokian, 1989.

Bibliography

Archives:

American Board of Commissioners for Foreign Missions, NY, US.A.

Archivio della sacra congregazione degli affari ecclesiastici straordinari, Citta di Vaticano.

Archivio Segreto Vaticano, Citta di Vaticano.

Deutscher Hilfsbund, Bad Homburg, Germany.

Eskijian Family Archives, Altadena CA., U.S.A.

Federal Archives, Military Archive, Freiburg, Germany

Foreign Office, Political Archive, Berlin, Germany.

Library of Congress, Washington, D.C., U.S.A.

Turkish Prime Minister's Ottoman Archives, Istanbul, Turkey.

Published Sources and Studies:

Adanýr, Fikret and Kaiser, Hilmar, "Migration, Deportation, and Nation-Building: the Case of the Ottoman Empire" in René Leboutte (ed.), *Migrations and Migrants in Historical Perspective. Permanencies and Innovations*, Bruxelles: Peter Lang, 2000 pp.273-292.

Allen, W. E. D. and Muratoff, Paul, *Caucasian Battlefields. A History of the Wars on the Turco-Caucasian Border, 1828-1921*, Cambridge: Cambridge University Press, 1953.

Andonian, Aram, *Documents officiels concernant les massacres arméniens*, translated by S. David-Beg, Paris: Imprimerie H. Turabian, 1920.

Askeri Tarih Belgeleri Dergisi 86 (1987).

Atkinson, Tacy, *"The German, the Turk and the Devil Made a Triple Alliance." Harpoot Diaries, 1908-1917*, (With a foreword by J. Michael Hagopian), Princeton, NJ: Gomidas Institute, 2000.

Barton, James L., *Story of Near East Relief (1915-1930). An Interpretation*, New York, NY: Macmillan, 1930.

Barton, James L. (compiler), *"Turkish Atrocities." Statements of American Missionaries on the Destruction of Christian Communities in Ottoman Turkey, 1915-1917*, Ann

Arbor, MI: Gomidas Institute, 1998.

Beylerian, Arthur (ed.), *Les grandes puissances, l'Empire ottoman et les Arméniens dans les archives françaises (1914-1918). Recueil de documents*, Paris: Publications de la Sorbonne (Série Documents, 34), 1983.

Bryce, James and Toynbee, Arnold, *The Treatment of Armenians in the Ottoman Empire, 1915-1916: Documents Presented to Viscount Grey of Fallodon by Viscount Bryce* [Uncensored Edition], (ed. and intro. by Ara Sarafian), Princeton, NJ: Gomidas Institute, 2000.

Cemal Paþa, *Hatýrâlar*, (ed. by Behçet Cemal), Istanbul: Selek Yayýnlarý, 1959.

Daniel, Robert L., *American Philanthropy in the Near East, 1820-1960*, Athens, Ohio: Ohio University Press, 1970.

Davidson, Khoren K., *Odysee of an Armenian of Zeitoun*. With a Foreword by Aram Saroyan, New York: Vantage Press, 1985.

Dinkel, Christoph, "Die schweizerische Armenierhilfe. Chronik von 1896 bis in die Zwischenkriegszeit" in Hans-Lukas Kieser (ed.), *Die armenische Frage und die Schweiz (1896-1923)*, Zürich: Chronos Verlag, 1999 pp.187-210.

Documents, [Ankara]; Prime Ministry, Directorate General of Press and Information, n.d.

Documents sur les Arméniens-Ottoman, vol. 2, [Ankara]: Présidence du conseil, Direction générale de la presse et de l'information, n.d.

Elmajian, Eflatoon E., *In the Shadow of the Almighty. My Life Story*, Pasadena, CA: n.p., 1982.

Erden, Ali Fuad, *Birinci Dünya Harbinde Suriye Hâtýralarý*, vol. 1, Istanbul: Halk Matbaasý, 1954.

Erickson, Edward J., *Ordered to Die. A History of the Ottoman in the First World War*, Westport, CT: The Greenwood Press (Contributions in Military Studies, no. 201) 2001.

Feigel, Uwe, *Das evangelische Deutschland und Armenien. Die Armenierhilfe deutscher evangelischer Christen seit dem Ende des 19. Jahrhunderts im Kontext der deutsch-türkischen Beziehungen*, Göttingen: Vandenhoeck & Ruprecht, (Kirche und Konfession, Band 28) 1989.

Gedenkschrift für Beatrice Rohner, Wüstenrot: Kurt Reith Verlag, 1947. Goekjian, Vahram K., *Voyage Through Stormy Seas. Part I: The Years of Peril and Bereavement*, New York, N.Y.: n.p., 1983.

Grabill, Joseph L., *Protestant Diplomacy and the Near East. Missionary Influence on American Policy, 1810-1927*, Minneapolis: University of Minnesota Press,

1971.

Hagobian-Taft, Elise, *Rebirth. The Story of an Armenian Girl Who Survived the Genocide and Found Rebirth in America*, Plandome, N.Y.: New Age Publishers, 1981.

Hartunian, Abraham H., *Neither To Laugh Nor To Weep*, transl. by Vartan Hartunian, 2nd ed. Intro. by Marjorie Housepian Dobkin, Boston, MA: NAASR, 1986.

His, Wilhelm, *Die Front der Ärzte,* Bielefeld: Velhagen und Klasing, 1931. His, Wilhelm, *Die Front der Ärzte,* Bielefeld: Velhagen und Klasing, 1931.

Impagliazzo, Marco, *Una finestra sul massacro. Documenti inediti sulla strage degli armeni (1915-1916)*, Milano: Guerini e Associati, 2000.

Ipek, Nedim, "Birinci Dünya Savaþ Esnasýnda Karadeniz ve Doðu-Anadolu'da Cereyan Eden Göçler" *19 Mayis ve Milli Mücadelede Samsun Sempozyumu*, Bildiriler, 16-20 Mayis 1994, Samsun, n.p., n.d.

Kaiser, Hilmar, "The Armenian Genocide: Governing Myths Revisited," paper presented at the 'Second Mediterranean Social and Political Research Meeting' European University Institute, Florence, March 21–25, 2001 (forthcoming).

Kaiser, Hilmar, "Amenian Property, Ottoman Law, and Nationality Policies During the Armenian Genocide, 1915-1915," paper presented at the International Workshop Ethnic Conflict and the Founding of the Turkish Republic, Rijksuniversiteit Leiden, May 17, 2000 (forthcoming).

Kaiser, Hilmar, "The Baghdad Railway and the Armenian Genocide, 1915-1916: A Case Study in German Resistance and Complicity" Richard G. Hovannisian (ed.), *Remembrance and Denial: The Case of the Armenian Genocide*, Detroit: Wayne State University Press, 1998 pp.67-112.

Kaiser, Hilmar, "Le génocide arménien: négation «à l'allemande»" *L' actualité du Génocide des Arméniens. Actes du colloque organisé par le Comité de Défense de la Cause Arménienne*, (Preface by Jack Lang), Paris: Edipol, 1999, pp.75-91.

Kaiser, Hilmar, "Dall'impero alla repubblica: le continuità del negazionismo turco" Marcello Flores (ed.) Milano: Bruno Mondadori, 2001.

Kazanjian, Paren (ed.), *The Cilician Armenian Ordeal*, Boston, MA: Hye Intentions Inc., 1989.

Kévorkian, Raymond, "Autres témoignages sur les déportations et les camps de concentration de Syrie et de Mésopotamie (1915-1916)," *Revue d'histoire arménienne contemporaine*, 2 (1998) pp.219-244.

Kévorkian, Raymond, "Le sort des déportés dans les camps de concentration de Syrie et de Mésopotamie," *Revue d'histoire arménienne contemporaine*, 2 (1998) pp.7-61.

Kévorkian, Raymond, "Témoignages sur les camps de concentration de Syrie et de Mésopotamie," *Revue d'histoire arménienne contemporaine*, 2 (1998) pp.62-215.

Kieser, Hans-Lukas (ed.), *Die armenische Frage und die Schweiz (1896-1923)*, Zürich: Chronos, 1999.

Kieser, Hans-Lukas, *Der verpasste Friede. Mission, Ethnie and Staat in den Ostprovinzen der Türkei 1839-1938*, Zürich: Chronos, 2000.

Kress von Kressenstein, Friedrich, *Mit den Türken zum Suezkanal. Erinnerungen eines deutschen Generalstabsoffiziers in türkischen Diensten*, Berlin: Vorhut-Verlag, 1938.

Litten, Wilhelm, *Persische Flitterwochen*, Berlin: Georg Stilke, 1925. Lührs, Hans, *Der Gegenspieler des Obersten Lawrence*, Berlin: Otto

Schlegel, 1936.

Miller, Donald E. and Touryan Miller, Lorna, *An Oral History of the Armenian Genocide*, Berkeley: California University Press, 1993.

Minassian, John, *Many Hills Yet to Climb. Memoirs of an Armenian Deportee*, Santa Barbara, CA: Jim Cook Publ., 1986.

Morley, Bertha B., *Marsovan 1915: The Diaries of Bertha Morley*, (ed. by Hilmar Kaiser), 2nd edition, Ann Arbor, MI: Gomidas Institute, 2000.

Mühlmann, Carl, *Oberste Heeresleitung und Balkan im Weltkrieg 1914/ 1918*, Berlin: Wilhelm Limpert Verlag, 1942.

Nesimi, Abidin, *Yýllarýn Ýçinden*, Istanbul: Gözlem Yayýnlarý, 1978.

Niepage, Martin, *The Horror's of Aleppo Seen by a German Eye-Witness*, London: T. Fisher Unwin, 1917.

Not by Bread Alone: The Life of Bertha B. Morley, written for her foster family, n.p.: College Press, 1967.

Orel, Þinasi and Yuca, Süreyya, *The Talât Pasha Telegrams. Historical Fact or Armenian Fiction?* Nicosia: K. Rustem & Brother, 1986.

Peet, Louise Jenison, *No Less Honor: The Biography of William Wheelock Peet*, n.p.: Privately Printed, 1939.

Riccardi, Andrea, *Il Mediterraneo. Cristianesimo e islam tra coabitazione e conflitto*, Milano: Guerini e Associati, 1997.

Riggs, Henry H., *Days of Tragedy in Armenia. Personal Experiences in Harpoot,*

1915-1917, Ann Arbor, MI: Gomidas Institute, 1997.

Rohner, Beatrice, *Die Stunde ist gekommen. Märtyrerbilder aus der Jetztzeit*, Frankfurt/M.: Verlag Orient, [1919].

Sarafian, Ara, "The Paper Trail: the American State Department and the Report of Committee on Armenian Atrocities," *Revue du monde arménien moderne et contemporain*, 1 (1994), pp.127-160.

Sarafian, Ara (compiler), *United States Official Documents on the Armenian Genocide*, Vols. 1-3, Watertown, MA: Armenian Review (Archival Collections on the Armenian Genocide) 1993-1995.

Saupp, Norbert, *Das Deutsche Reich und die Armenische Frage 1878-1914*, PhD dissertation, University of Köln, 1990.

Schilling, Viktor, *Kriegshygienische Erfahrungen in der Türkei (Cilicien, Nordsyrien)*, Leipzig: J. A. Barth, (Beihefte zum Archiv für Schiffs- und Tropenhygiene, Bd. 25) 1921.

Shepard Riggs, Alice, *Shepard of Aintab*, New York, N.Y.: Interchurch Press, 1920.

Simon, Hyacinthe, *Mardine. La ville heroïque. Autel et tombeau de l'Arménie (Asie Mineure) durant les massacres de 1915*, edited by Naji Naaman, introduction by Georges Yeghiayan, Jounieh: Maison Naaman pour la culture, 1991.

Soulahian Kuyumjian, Rita, *Archeology of Madness. Komitas, Portrait of an Icon*, Princeton, N.J.; Gomidas Institute, 2001.

Sutherland, James K., *Adventures of an Armenian Boy. Reminiscences of Dr. James K. Sutherland*, Ann Arbor, MI: The Ann Arbor Press, 1964.

Ter Minassian, Anahide, "Un exemple, Mouch 1915" *L'actualité du Génocide des Arméniens. Actes du colloque organisé par le Comité de Défense de la Cause Arménienne*, (preface by Jack Lang), Paris: Edipol, 1999 pp.231-252.

Ter Minassian, Anahide Anahide, "Van 1915" in Richard G. Hovannisian (ed.), *Armenian Van/Vaspurakan*, Costa Mesa, CA: Mazda Publishers (UCLA Armenian History and Culture Series, Historic Armenian Cities and Provinces, 1) 2000, pp.209-244.

Trumpener, Ulrich, *Germany and the Ottoman Empire, 1914 - 1918*, Princeton, NJ: Princeton University Press, 1968; reprint, Delmar, NY: Caravan Books, 1989.

Türkiye Cumhuriyeti, Baþbakanlýk Devlet Arþivleri Genel Müdürlüðü, Osmanlý Arþivi Daire Bakanlýðý, *Osmanlý Belgelerinde Ermeniler (1915-1920)*, Ankara: Baþbakanlýk Basýmevi, 1994.

Von der Goltz, Colmar, *Denkwürdigkeiten*, ed. by. Friedrich Von der Goltz and

Wolfgang Foerster, Berlin: Mittler & Sohn, 1929.

Von Gleich, Gerold, *Vom Balkan nach Bagdad. Militärisch-politische Erinnerungen an den Orient*, Berlin: Otto Scherl, 1921.

Weber, Frank G., *Eagles on the Crescent. Germany, Austria and the Diplomacy of the Turkish Alliance, 1914-1918*, Ithaca, Cornell University Press, 1970.

White, George E., *Adventuring with Anatolia College*, Grinnell, Iowa: Herald-Register Publishing Company, 1940.

Wolffskeel von Reichenberg, Eberhard, *Zeitoun, Mousa Dagh, Ourfa. Letters on the Armenian Genocide*, (ed. and intro. by Hilmar Kaiser), Princeton, NJ: Gomidas Institute, 2001.